The Process

Mental Training and the Principles of Limitless Golfing Success

Written By Jon Levitt

FOREWORD
By Bill McKinney, PGA

Being simultaneously a golf geek and a little bit of a neurotic bookworm, I make it a point to read plenty of technical studies and books in hopes of making my job as a player and a golf instructor a little bit easier. As we all know, the *It factor* isn't nearly as physical as it is mental. There are hundreds of books and mental coaches who offer their services. Myself, I have the good fortune to be the "Swing Coach" to 3 very highly rated college players at the moment who all received advance copies of this book as part of their strategy to continue to not only guard their talent, but to nurture it to full bloom. Jon's book, *The Process*, is a refreshingly user-friendly guidebook that is also loaded with anecdotes from his own "tin cup" career as a journeyman pro golfer. It is a confidential of sorts that reminds me of the way old-school strength coaches write about getting big and strong--no BS, just work hard on the simple and solid basics that have proven to work over the years, and cut the fat. Most importantly, it is simply a good solid plan to keep your mental fortress secure and tidy. Over-thinking is easily the worst trap into which we striving golfers fall.

I have played hundreds of rounds with Jon, and he's not exaggerating in his quips about keeping his scores between mid 60's to low 70's while making it look pretty vanilla-like. I have been preaching vanilla golf for my own star students for the last 10 years now. It is powerfully liberating to play with the Process he has mapped out.

Neither is he exaggerating about the way he evolved from a self-centered competitor to a wizened and, dare I say, pleasant fellow competitor who always knows how to help a struggling friend with a small bit of advice that seems to clear the dark clouds. I believe it was there all along, he was just such a good competitor that he kept his secrets to himself.

We often discussed for hours after a round or over a beer or two, the principles of successful golfing. He confided in me some of the secrets he kept from his fellow competitors, which altered my approach to certain aspects of the game.

There are plenty of golf psychology books, but there are too few written from the vantage point of a professional player with the intellectual pedigree that Jon possesses. His father, being a Ph.D. Sports Psychologist and scratch golfer himself, literally used his son as a proving ground for the powers of what eventually became his book, *The*

Process. Jon was raised on sports psychology and used it in every sport he played--and was at least proficient if not excellent in all of them! His evolution into a humble and generous mentor came with age, years of reading, soul-searching (and maybe a little good-natured ribbing from his friends).

Use this book as a roadmap or a reference book. It will help keep your sanity in an imperfect game invented by some crazy Scottish shepherds who were probably drunk off their kilts and having a laugh along the glacier carved natural fairways. Little did they know what a can of worms they were opening for so many generations of golfers.
I am proud to be the one to write the foreword for this powerful book, *The Process*. Stick to it and you will succeed.

Bill McKinney, PGA
2011 Metro Chapter SCPGA Teacher of the Year
www.swingfitgolf.com

INTRODUCTION

If you look in the golf section aisle of any bookstore, you'll find dozens of books claiming to increase your power or add twenty yards to your driver. A few dozen more claiming to fix your slice or teach you the finer points of chipping or putting. You might also find a book or two about the mysterious mental game of golf, which is where you most likely stumbled upon this book.

The books about your swing or the mechanics of the game are important but there is something that is often neglected by even the most talented golfers. Without a sound fundamental mental process, all the books on swing mechanics, chipping, and putting are of little use.

As a golf instructor, I would often have students say to me, "I subscribe to magazines on golf, have a hundred golf books, and many DVD's from famous instructors, but I'm not sure which one works the best? What should I do?" Usually I tell them to start a fire and throw it all in! *Too much information for the untrained golfer can often cause more damage than it does good.*

I am considered an expert on all subjects pertaining to golf but too much information can even be a problem for me. So I can only imagine what is going on in the mind of the student with information overload.

I do love to learn everything I can about the game. I have read books on every aspect of the game. I enjoy the books on the subject of the mental game of golf most of all. They are interesting to me and all have some useful information but lack one critical criteria, functional experience. Psychology is an amazingly complex topic which requires years of education and research. Let's face it though, there is no substitute for experience.

If you were hunting in the forest and out of nowhere an angry Grizzly Bear charged at you. I'm sure a psychologist would say in that situation to take a deep breath, steady your nerves, aim your rifle at the bears heart and squeeze the trigger with confidence. The problem is that this psychologist has never faced down a charging Grizzly Bear before and has no idea what is going through your head at that particular moment.

Another example I like to use is walking across a plank on the ground as opposed to walking across the same plank 100 feet in the air. No one would think twice about walking across the plank on the ground because there is nothing to fear, but raise that plank twenty feet in the air and you're going to have a fear of hurting yourself. Raise the plank 1000 feet above ground and very few would dare try for fear of death.

Someone could tell you how to compose yourself and focus on placing one foot in front of the other, or how to channel your focus in a way as to not look down. But unless you've walked across that 1000 foot high plank, you have no idea what is going on in the head of the person giving it a try.

It doesn't mean that what they told you isn't the correct way to proceed, but what if their lack of experience causes them to miss one crucial point that hasn't entered their thought because they've never been there before. The missing detail might lead to failure and in these examples, a horrible death! Golf won't kill you physically but without the right Process, it can seem at times like mentally it will.

Here is a little about me and why I am different from those who will tell you how to react or behave without actually having the experience. I know what you're going through because I have metaphorically been in the forest and faced down the charging bears and walked across the highest planks.

I didn't get serious with golf until I was about 15 years old. I played all the sports that young athletic boys play early in life. I excelled mainly at basketball, but also played football, baseball, tennis, and just about any other game that got my competitive juices flowing. I loved the thrill of competition, even from a very early age.

I grew up with three rather non-athletic brothers, so I had to seek out games throughout the Southern

California neighborhood I grew up in. In high school I was on the basketball team but didn't really have the discipline to listen to a coach I felt knew little about the game and teammates that didn't have a desire to win at all costs, like I did.

My father was a scratch golfer and a psychologist with a Ph.D in clinical psychology. He was an expert on *Stress Management*. He wrote a book on the subject and even appeared on the "Phil Donahue Show" in the 80's discussing his book.

From an early age, I think he saw the potential I had to become a successful athlete. He, unknowingly to me, was imparting his new found love of sports psychology into everything I was doing in my athletic endeavors. He would say some of the same things over and over to me as I continued to excel in any given activity. I would tell him I knew someone was cheating and he would say, "Winners never cheat and cheaters never win". If I ever talked about the past he would say, "Stay in the moment". If it appeared that I wasn't focused, he would impart deep concepts like "Find your center and focus on your target".

I remember playing basketball games as a kid and hearing him yell when I was about to shoot a free throw, "Don't forget to breathe". Thanks for that Dad, I'll remember to breathe! My friends had looks on their faces like, "Is your dad an idiot?" It was a little embarrassing. Sports psychology hadn't quite made its way into the mainstream in the 70's, but he was confident that one day the foundation he was laying for my future athletic career would pay off. He taught me the physical aspects of golf by basically saying, "Here are some balls, here's how you hold the club, and here's how you swing, now have fun and leave me alone! If you have trouble just watch me." I think he saw my natural ability and didn't feel he knew enough about swing mechanics to really add to what I already possessed (or he just didn't want me bothering him). His focus with me was to train my mind to compete at any level. Not to be concerned with whether my left arm was straight or if I made a complete shoulder turn.

He never really pushed me to do anything, I guess he figured that with my stubborn nature, if he pushed me I would lose interest. He was probably right. I think though that somewhere there has to be a happy medium between pushing too hard and not pushing enough. I struggle with that today with my own daughter.

In high school, I had two friends who were fantastic golfers, the Higgins brothers. Chuck and Tim were great guys and they did have a little athletic ability, but I could easily beat them in a 2-on-1 basketball game. On the golf course though, that was a different story. They would humiliate me out there. Being a fierce competitor, that didn't sit well with me. The Higgins boys got me a job caddying at a local country club and thus began my lifelong love affair with the great game of golf.

I worked every day on my game and excelled rapidly. I tried out for the golf team my junior year of high school and played fifth man on my team. By my senior year, I had improved so fast that I was the number one man on the team and had a fairly good year. The golf bug had hit me pretty hard by then and I was looking for a college to play for. I hadn't done enough to gain the attention of any college coaches and couldn't afford to go to a major university, so I enrolled at a junior college and played a successful year there.

It was in that year of JC golf that got me enough recognition from some golf coaches, that I was offered a golf scholarship to play for a four year university. I had a pretty decent college career and was voted to the All-American team in division II golf my senior year in 1986.

The thought of playing golf professionally never entered my mind until about three years after I graduated. I kept my game up by playing in as many amateur tournaments as possible but it wasn't until I got a job as a teaching pro that I started to think about playing the game as a professional.

I got a very late start to the world of professional golf, as I didn't turn pro until I was 26 years old. Though I was tall, strong, and very athletic, I wasn't the guy who was super long off the tee or fantastically skilled in all aspects of the game. What I did have was a head start on the mental side of the game that most players either never attain or only read a book about because someone tells them they should.

I turned professional in 1989 and began playing the mini-tours in California. In my first five tournaments, I had two wins, two seconds, and a third. It seemed very easy to me...and then I got married. Golf wasn't so easy anymore. I began to feel guilty about playing. Over time *I allowed* my ex-wife to take the fun out of the game for me. "When are you going to get a real job!" was a phrase I heard a hundred times. It was really soul crushing. Once this game (or anything that you love) gets into your every fiber, make sure you surround yourself with people who truly believe in you and support your dream.

After a relatively painless divorce, my career took off. For the first time in four years I was on the golf course enjoying myself. No worries or guilty feelings and a true appreciation and love for what I was doing.

The wins came more frequently and it was then that I decided to fully devote myself to the *pursuit* of perfection in golf and my life (not the attainment of perfection itself, which is an important distinction). I began to develop my physical and mental approach to the game. I read everything on the subject of the psychology of the game. I read so much that I discovered it was the reading itself that strengthened my mind and made me a better player. I even began to read about spiritual and meditative approaches to life and how I could apply those teachings to my own golf game.

It was that burning quest for knowledge that led me to a relatively successful journey and career in the game of golf. I played all over the world on a few different tours, such as the U.S. Nike Tour (now the Nationwide Tour), the South American PGA Tour (Tour de las Americas), and the Asian PGA Tour. I've won over 40 tournaments as a pro and I played in the 2000 U.S. Open at Pebble Beach.

At age 49, I am now working with young talented players, imparting some wisdom of the mental aspects that I've accumulated over the years. Without these methods of the mental approach, I think it's next to impossible to achieve success at the highest levels. As you will read in this book, I have broken down and organized my thoughts and put them into a *Process* that can be followed step by step to help you attain any goals you have set for yourself.

Though I grew up with my father's teachings, studied psychology in college, read extensively on every aspect of the subject, and devoted my life to implementing my own mental training in everything I do, I am not a Ph.D. What I do have that almost no *Mental Trainer* has though, is the experience of playing in more than 500 tournaments and standing before tens of thousands of spectators watching me hit a golf ball. Until you've walked a mile in a man's shoes, it's hard to understand what's going on in his head. I know what's going on in your head when you're on the golf course because I've been there. A close friend of mine, playing devil's advocate, asked me "Why would anyone listen to you, you're not a famous golfer or sports psychologist?" I could have told him all the "excuses" that kept me from achieving success on the PGA Tour. My late start to pro golf, the chronically bad back that plagued my entire career, my desire at the time to, let's say, enjoy life a little too much or the fact that though I used *a process* to my mental approach as a pro, it wasn't the organized *Process* and methods to mental training you are going to read about, would have been an acceptable answer for him.

Instead, I chose to explain to him that I was tired of reading mental training books about golf written by people without practical experience. To only be able to assume what was going on in a person's mind in a stressful situation isn't the same thing as knowing it from actual experience. I devoted 30 years of my life to not just the competition of the game, but *every* aspect of this beautiful and complicated sport. Along the way I made a lot of mistakes and I am writing this book to help all of you avoid the same pitfalls. I only wish I had someone with this kind of knowledge to help me when I started to play the game more seriously. Maybe I would have made better decisions which would have led to a more prosperous career or at least a greater enjoyment of the game. You won't hear this information from the players on tour because they want to beat you. It is an unwritten law out there that each player keeps the secrets of their success to themselves. They simply don't want you to know what they know. What I hope you get from this book and my training techniques are an understanding of how your mind works and how to make it work positively for you in any given situation. A set, easy to follow Process that can be repeated even in times of stress that will bring a calmness and consistency that you've never experienced before. Plus a real belief that by following this Process it will make you a much better golfer (and if it's possible, to be a happier and healthier person).

You may find some of the theories in the book complex but please don't feel that you must master every aspect to improve your game. Pick and choose what works for you. Keep reading the book and eventually, I feel confident you will grasp all concepts and should get at least a general understanding of every chapter in the book.

By the time you feel you've implemented everything I've written about, you should already be well on your way to achieving some or all of the goals you've set for yourself. Then it's time to set new and exciting goals and you will have a belief that those new goals will be within your reach.

Some students take to the Process like a proverbial duck to water. For others it will be a bit more challenging. But all who put in the time will be amazed at the positive changes in their game and maybe in their life as well. So don't despair if it takes time get a grasp of some of these concepts, because the Process is an ongoing venture that lasts a lifetime. Some aspects will work immediately for you but others will take a lifetime to fully understand, attain, or possibly, perfect. The beauty is that life is a journey and should be enjoyed no matter how long it takes for you to understand it.

The good news is that golf, unlike most sports we play in our youth, can be played well into our golden years. Following the Process will help make that journey so much more enjoyable and enable you to reach goals you thought to be previously unattainable.

In the book you'll learn the proper pre-shot routine, both physically and mentally. You'll learn the concept of acceptance and all the good inner feelings that come from it. You'll learn proper focus techniques and tools such as self-hypnosis and meditation to assist you with your focus. You'll learn how to apply the Process during play and how to handle the biggest moments. And you'll learn how to manage your life more effectively off the course so you'll be better prepared on the course.

After completing this book you will be ready to incorporate the principles of the Process into your everyday life and golf will become exactly what it's meant to be...Fun!

There is one last thing that is important to understand before you begin reading, this book is for ALL golfers. I do tend to speak specifically to those aspiring to reach the highest achievements in the game but *The Process* works for any golfer. Male or female, young or old, and players of any skill level.

In fact, it's the beginner who will find the fastest positive results because they haven't yet developed the ingrained habits of the experienced golfer. It's these developed habits that are the hardest to let go of at times. But when you begin to see the benefits of the Process, you will be amazed at how quickly your game will improve and how much easier and more fun you will have playing the greatest of all games, Golf.

Good golfing, and enjoy *The Process*.

Chapter 1

PRE-SHOT ROUTINE:
The Engine of the Process

Golf is a game of repetition. The most successful at it are the ones who can most consistently repeat their actions over and over again. Sure we need a fundamentally sound golf swing, a reliable short game and a pure putting stroke, but how do we come by those? Through correct repetition!

Since golf is one of the most challenging of all sports, an enormous amount of work and practice are required to achieve success at any level.

It's here where I feel the need to be honest with you. Golf is loaded with mental and physical pitfalls on the road to success. If you want to succeed at the highest level, you better be prepared to put in the hard work and develop the correct Process. Because let me tell you, every one of the best players in the world is putting everything they have into becoming the best. So if you're not willing to put in the work, you may have to prepare for a bumpy road.

Now there are many levels of golfing ability and competition. If your goal is to beat your buddies in a weekend round of golf, read this book, devote as much time as you can to the practice of it and they won't have a chance against you. If your goals are somewhat loftier, say the PGA Tour, then yes, you'll have to dedicate your life to exhaustive daily physical and mental training. Fortunately, this is some of the most fun work you could possibly do. Let's begin by discussing one of the most important things to any player; A fundamental pre-shot routine.

If you watch golf on TV and you are really observant, you'll see that every player has a distinctive pre-shot routine that they repeat every time. This is one reason why you are watching them on TV. Remember, golf is a game of repetition. It is crucial that before every single shot you hit, you are approaching it the same way. It doesn't have to be like anybody else's routine but it always has to be the same for you.

Why is a pre-shot routine so important?
Golf is different from most sports in that the ball is not moving when you hit. You have time to analyze your situation and proceed when you are ready. The proper preparation is essential for success. Do a different preparation every time and you will undoubtedly get a different result every time. You want to approach every shot the same way, because you want the results to be the same.
Of course you could do the same thing every time and still have unsuccessful results. Nobody is perfect and we're going to have to accept some

imperfect shots, but the main point is that your chances of excellence are greater with the proper preparation.

What is the proper pre-shot routine?
There is no one correct way. The most important point to remember is that you follow the same routine every time. Here are four suggestions to follow:

1) Analyze your situation.
Figure out your distance based on all the conditions such as wind, altitude, weather, slope, etc. Assess the best place for your shot to end up and how to shape your shot. Select the club you feel best fits the shot you want to hit, and select it with confidence.

2) Imagine with all five senses how you want to hit the shot (explained in chapter on Focus)

3) Rehearse the shot with one, two, or three practice swings which exactly replicate the swing you would want to make while actually hitting the shot. (*Again remember, it doesn't matter how many rehearsals you make, as long as you do the same thing every time in your pre-shot routine.*)

4) ALWAYS ask yourself if you are ready to hit this shot! Meaning, are you comfortable with your analysis of the situation? Do you feel like you have the right club in your hands? Are you aimed correctly? Are your thoughts clear and confident? Is anything distracting you?

If your answer is "Yes I'm ready to hit a great shot", then proceed with confidence. If there is any reason why you might hesitate, stop and go through the process all over again, until the answer is "Yes I'm ready...".

Padraig Harrington once told a reporter, "If I never once changed my mind or doubted myself over the ball, I'd win every week."

Believe it or not, you can do all of those four steps in a matter of seconds. It does require practice but the more you perfect this routine, the less times you'll feel uncertain over the ball. The more certain you are over the ball the higher will be your success rate.

It's important to note that over analysis of the situation can be as destructive as under analysis. Keep your routine as simple, yet effective as possible. I'm sure you've heard the saying "Paralysis through analysis". This paralysis happens when there are so many things going through our head that we overload the mind with unnecessary thoughts and confuse the body's natural fluidity.

There must be a connection between the mind and body that allows them to work equally for the best completion of the task at hand.

A good friend of mine suffers from the affliction of over analysis. His golf game is painfully slow. He does have a relatively consistent pre-shot routine but it takes forever to execute. He stands over the ball and you can see the wheels spinning in his head. He takes too many practice swings that aren't rehearsal swings, he just flails the club back and through almost as if to loosen up his body. Then he stands over the ball endlessly waggling the club and I'm sure he's going through a long list of mechanical swing thoughts. Finally he pulls the trigger and more often than not he produces an offline miss hit.

The saddest thing is that he is an incredibly intelligent man and a very gifted athlete, capable of playing so much better. It's my belief that he *allows* his intelligence to negatively affect his game. He just thinks too much and the connection between his mind and his body are completely out of sync. On the range after one of his particularly difficult rounds, I begged him to try hitting a shot using my pre-shot routine. He stubbornly argued that his routine works. I asked him to humor me one time and do exactly what I say. It was almost painful for him but he tried it.

The first two attempts, he couldn't (or was just too stubborn to) do the routine exactly the way I asked.

On the third try he actually followed my instructions to stand behind the ball, pick a target, visualize the flight of the intended shot, step into position and take one practice swing exactly rehearsing the intended shot, address the ball, take one last look at the target, ask himself if he was ready to hit the shot, and pull the trigger.

He hit his best shot of the day by far. He tried it again just to make sure it wasn't a fluke and again a beautifully struck shot directly at the target. And again. And again. I smiled and explained to him that the game isn't as difficult as he was making it. Yet, as I walked away I looked back to see him going back to his old routine. Not surprisingly, he produced more poor shots. Some people are just their own worst enemy.

So remember, the ball isn't moving and you have a lot of time to think before you hit it. With the proper pre-shot routine, your mind will only be focused on the few things required to hit a great shot, instead of the thousands of things that can pop into your head which can often lead to a disastrous result.

The Rule of 1000

As a part of analyzing any shot, I often use what I call "The rule of 1000". This is a relatively simple concept to anyone who has played the game for years but for younger or inexperienced players, this concept can be confusing. Basically it means that if you were to play the shot before you 1000 times, what would be the best course of strategy for that particular situation.

Here is an example. You are 175 yards away from the hole, in the middle of the fairway. The hole is on the left side of the green, 15 feet away from a lake. There is sand short of the green (I would say sand trap or bunker, but the terms *trap* or *bunker* are negative words which should be avoided), and lots of green right of the hole. Here is where you would start to analyze the situation with the rule of 1000. If you were to play the hole by hitting 1000 shots directly at the flag or 1000 shots at the center of the green, which would produce the lowest score averaged out over 1000 attempts.

Let's say that by attacking the flag, you made 100 double bogeys because you pulled shots into the water, made 200 bogeys because of water or sand problems, made 400 birdies because you hit it close and made the putts, and made 300 pars because you two putted. That would give you and average score of level par for a 1000 attempts.

If you played conservatively and aimed for the middle of the green, you might hit 900 of those shots on the green, but you would have an average putt of about 15 to 20 feet. Let's say you make 150 of those 900 attempts, three putt 30 of them, and maybe leave 50 in the front sand and get half of those up and down for par and bogeying the other 25. Another 50 you miss the green and 30 of those up and down and 20 bogeys. that's a total of 75 under par for 1000 attempts. So in that scenario, hitting for the middle of the green would be the best statistical play.

I know what you're thinking; "I'm not a mathematician, and that would take forever to figure out even if I was!". Actually, I can do it in a matter of seconds and when you do it enough, so will you. A lot of times it's a gut feeling. You know in an instant what feels right and most every time you should go with you first instinct. But when it's an *either/or* situation, use the rule of 1000 to help you make the final decision.

There are occasions when there are exceptions to the rule. If you are one shot down with one hole to play, I would recommend being aggressive and attacking any pin. If you absolutely know that you can pull the shot off, give it a go. If you feel that you need to stay aggressive or to take a chance in that moment, then proceed with absolute confidence. Some players never hear the end of it when laying up or playing safe (not that I would ever recommend listening to arm chair quarterbacks). As long as you can live with whatever decision you make, then you have most likely made a good decision.

Another reason why you can do this quicker than you might think is that you have been in this same situation a 1000 times and you will almost instinctually know which approach will work the best.

For the inexperienced or younger player who haven't been in certain situations enough times, I would recommend the *rule of 10,* as it works almost the same. But for the experienced player, 10 times doesn't quite factor in all the possible outcomes. Though knowing the importance of situational strategy analysis, I would advise against bogging yourself down with thoughts that are too confusing. The overload of thoughts may be more detrimental than a good strategy can be beneficial.
Practicing the rule of 1000 will make it much less confusing and more practical with your situational analysis, but one important key to the game is to keep things as simple as possible.
Every shot requires some form of analysis but most times, even for the beginner, the answer is obvious. A ten foot putt, straight in and uphill doesn't require the rule of 1000. All that is required is to pick your line, gather the right speed, and knock that ball in the back of the cup. You don't need to know what the consequences are of a ten foot putt. It's when you are on the fence as whether to hit a driver off or three wood off the tee and the results might be

relatively similar, that is when the use of the rule of 1000 is so helpful.

Correct decision making can make all the difference in a round of golf or in life. The best way to make a correct decision is to have as many accurate facts as possible and to have a strategy based on the proper analysis of those facts. By analyzing the situation properly you'll be able to proceed with confidence and your chances for success will increase.

Ever go into an exam completely unprepared and think "I'm going to ace this test"? Probably not. When you study all the information and prepare properly, you walk into that same exam with a confidence knowing that your chances of success are high. It's a good feeling. Every shot in the game of golf is like a test and the better prepared we are, the better are our chances of a good outcome. Again it's important to note that there are times when we over study for a test. We fill our head with so much information that confusion sets in. Learn what facts are important to a particular situation. Assess the situation, go through your routine, and proceed with confidence, but try not to over analyze.

Chapter 2

ACCEPTANCE:
The Heart of the Process

Depending on your personality, acceptance may be the most difficult lesson you learn from this book. As a youth, my competitive nature was as aggressive as anyone's. I absolutely hated to lose and was very hard on myself when I made what I would perceive to be a mistake. I would even lose sleep after a particularly difficult loss, especially if I felt I was to blame.

It took me many years to learn to accept the results of my actions. I still hate to lose, but I have now learned to accept it with grace and humility.

I've heard that in the game of golf there can only be one winner. I couldn't disagree more. Our goal should always be to play our best. Therefore, if we do truly play our best and we are bested, did we really lose? It's certainly debatable but I don't think so.

One expression I use a lot with my students (and in this book) is "Golf is a marathon, not a sprint". Don't let one shot, or one tournament, or even one disappointing year bring you down. If you shoot a round of 60 and someone else shoots 59, would you consider yourself a loser? Well if you did, you would be missing the point. I would much rather play the best round of my life and finish second than play poorly and win. Keep shooting rounds like that and you will eventually finish first. The people who can learn from their defeats and move on in a positive direction are the true champions.

The concept of acceptance works particularly well with individual shots. For example, you hit a ball into the trees and upon arrival at the ball, you see that you are behind a tree. It is at this point that most golfers start to piss and moan about how unlucky they are, or that this wouldn't happen to anyone else, or a dozen other negative thoughts.

With acceptance, you can look at that situation and think, "This is an opportunity for greatness" or at the very least, "Hey, I'm the one who hit it here in the first place, so let's make the best of it." Accept it and move on with a positive attitude.

Golf, viewed as a sprint, could make it very tough to accept certain breaks or situations. It could even seem unfair at times. How often do you think, "All the ball had to do was bounce a little to the right but it bounced hard to the left directly behind the tree." These things happen all the time on the course and after seemingly endless rounds of perceived *bad* breaks, your blood can reach a boiling point.

Even the most saintly among us can completely lose their cool on the course, but this book will give you techniques that will make it unnecessary to even think about losing your cool. They say that golf is a game that reveals your true personality. Does that have to mean revealing what a jerk you are? Let's face it, most all of us have lost our cool in the heat of battle, and when we do, we all looked like spoiled little crybabies.

A friend of mine who is a bit of a hot head used to tell me, "I have to let off a little steam every now and then or I'll completely blow up!" I would tell him, "If your approach to the game was correct, you would never have any steam that needs to be let off." Learn to accept every situation with grace and confidence and this game will become so much easier.

Anger is a poison that has ruined many a round of golf. It is the cause of ulcers, high blood pressure, unhappiness, broken golf clubs, and it makes you look foolish and out of control.

Some believe that they play better when they are angry. In my experience this is never true. What they mean is that their focus intensifies when they get mad. That never lasts and it usually leads to even worse outbursts and bigger mistakes. It's always better to find ways to have intense focus without the anger.

The other thing about playing with anger or impatience is that it takes you out of the moment. There is only one place where you can be successful and that is in the moment. Anger, fear, and impatience are all emotions based in the past and future but rarely in the present. Acceptance, if done properly is found in the present. You're not worried about what's going to happen or why you always get such perceived *bad* breaks. The only thought in your head is what to do right now in this moment. What just happened or what's going to happen are beyond your control, but what you're going to do about it right now is a very empowering feeling.

Yes, there is a lot of power in the moment. Past and future negative thoughts can be very draining on the psyche. Concentrating only on the task at hand can give you the full positive energy required to proceed with confidence.

PATIENCE AND YOUR PATH

Of all the personality characteristics required to be a successful golfer, patience is the most functional. Golf is loaded with many land mines of impatience. It's most noticeable in the plague of slow play. Waiting for three groups to hit on a hole is painful. Slow play can throw you off your rhythm, tighten up your muscles, and be just plain aggravating.

The funny thing about patience though, is that it's not something that can be switched on just by saying "I'm just going to be patient now". That simply won't work. Patience requires training, just as acceptance does. Later on I'll go into the proper breathing, meditation, and off course methods that are required to build your patience level...you'll just have to read on and be patient!

What I can tell you about my own life long struggle with patience is that the more you work on it, the easier it becomes. Growing up as one of the better all around athletes in my town and being a fiercely intense competitor, I had a difficult time dealing with the kids that couldn't keep up. I didn't make a lot of friends because of my lack of patience. As a leader on the field, I wouldn't hesitate to yell at those who didn't pull their weight. I learned the hard way that the quest for perfection was a lonely one.

Ironically, it was my impatience with and my intolerance for inferior teammates that led me to golf. Nobody to get mad at but myself. You know the expression, "Be careful what you wish for, for you just might get it!". Well I got it. With no one else to direct my rage at, I got mad at myself quite often. Impatient and angry is no way to succeed at anything or to enjoy your life.

My impatience got so bad that I lost interest in the game for a short time in my early twenties. Then I got married and had a baby. If you ever want to test your patience, get married and have a baby! My daughter, Gabriela, was and is the love of my life, but she stretched my patience daily. One minute I would look down at that cute little girl and think,

"How could I love anything more than this beautiful baby!" and the next minute I was wondering what had I got myself into.

She liked to cry, wake up at all hours of the night, and was an amazingly finicky eater. My nerves were frayed. I regained my love for golf because it was a refuge from the noise and stress of everyday life. The golf course was a peaceful place where I could hide from my problems. I didn't learn until years later that she wasn't the problem, I was.

I continued spiraling down a dark road. My marriage was failing and I was miserable. I had turned professional at age 26 and was still playing decent golf but I had never been unhappier. I *allowed* others to make me feel guilty for doing what I loved to do, play golf.

My marriage finally ended after four years and I again felt like I had failed because my daughter was going to be brought up in a broken home, just as her mother and father were. I had hit rock bottom. I remember the day like it was yesterday when I decided to make a radical change in my life.

I went on a two year long journey to find peace, clarity, and a cleansing of my psyche. I studied such things as spirituality, meditation, and self-hypnosis. I read books on religion, philosophy, and psychology. I learned everything I could about gaining peace of mind, obtaining patience, and what it took to be kind and generous with others.

After years of my personal quest for tranquility, I found what I was looking for: *Happiness.*

Things that used to bother me no longer even caught my attention. I had changed my personality and character so much, that people I would run into after not seeing for a few years would always ask, "Where is the guy I used to know, and what have you done with him?". It was a backhanded compliment of sorts, but it was nice to hear that all my very hard transformational work was apparent to others.

I did often wonder, was it because I had become such a noticeably decent person or that I was just such a rotten asshole before that any positive change would be noticeable? It didn't really matter, as long as I was going in the right direction. And I was. I had the patience of Job and life was so easy that almost nothing could obstruct my path. It's my objective that after you read this book you will have your own clear path to follow.

My favorite line from the classic book "Alice in Wonderland" is when Alice, lost in the forest, comes across the Cheshire Cat. She says, "Excuse me sir, but can you help me? I'm lost". He asks "Where do you want to go?" She says "I don't know", and he replies "Then it really doesn't matter *which* way you go!".

If you don't know where you want to go, then it really doesn't matter which way you go. Have a destination, find your transportation, take the most direct path to your goals, and don't let anything get in the way of your path.

THE FINE LINE BETWEEN SUCCESS AND FAILURE

Another flaw most golfers have is their judgmental nature. To most, every shot is determined to be either *good* or *bad*. Judgments in everyday life can actually save your life. It's probably a good judgment not to go down a dark alley at night in a dangerous neighborhood. Usually though, it's judgments that get us in trouble or have us miss out on amazing opportunities. "Never judge a book by its cover" is a phrase we've all heard but advice we rarely follow. Some judgments even lead to certain prejudices.

We all hit shots that don't go where we want them to. I believe that is because we are human and human's aren't perfect. Accept it and move on. To constantly judge every shot as good or bad makes you focus on the results and not the process. There is such a fine line between what is good or bad that it's always better to just focus on the Process. If you have a 15 foot putt and you read it to break six inches left to right, and you hit it perfectly on the line you read with the right speed, and the putt only breaks four inches and lips out, was that good or bad? Was it a success or a failure? By my definition, if you do exactly what you were trying to do then that was a successful attempt. Just because the result of your intention wasn't met doesn't mean a thing.

Greg Norman felt he never hit a *bad* putt. In his mind good putts that didn't go in were usually because of a mis-read.

We have no control over the result, so to even judge anything based on the results is futile. If you do exactly what your trying to do on any given shot, the result is inconsequential.

Keep doing things the way you're trying to and eventually things will go your way. There is definitely something to be said for doing your very best. Sometimes the most important thing to understand the day after a round of golf is that you have the peace of mind in knowing that you gave your best on every shot, win or lose.

NEW OPPORTUNITIES FOR GREATNESS

Sometimes with acceptance comes challenges. When your shot goes out of bounds, in the lake, behind a tree, in a divot in the middle of the fairway, etc., that's when you'll gain strength in acceptance and patience. Look upon these perceived challenges as new opportunities for greatness. There is nothing more rewarding to your psyche than to handle a difficult situation with poise and dignity.

Early in my professional career I entered a PGA Tour Monday qualifier for the San Diego Open. I played an excellent round and ended up in a two-for-one playoff to see who would play in the tournament. We both birdied the first hole, and then on the second playoff hole, I learned a painful lesson about acceptance.

The hole was a reachable 4 par with trouble on both sides. A classic risk/reward golf hole. My competitor hit a really nice drive which landed in front of the green and bounced just right of the sand and onto the green about twenty feet away for eagle. I hit the identical shot with the ball landing in nearly the exact same spot. My ball though, bounced just to the left and into the sand. I'm an exceptional sand player, but with a hundred attempts I couldn't have placed one ball closer than 15 feet from the hole. I did hit the best possible shot to about 15 feet.

My opponent two putted and I had to make my putt to continue the match. I hadn't yet let go of the unfortunate bounce of my ball into the sand, but I tried to focus and make the putt. I made a confident stroke and the ball caught part of the hole, but didn't go in.

I think it took me about two months to emotionally recover from that qualifier. I wanted so badly to play in that tournament that I let it affect my play for that period of time. Eventually I let it go and because I learned so much from that event, I decided to use it as my stepping stone into formulating the basic foundation of acceptance within The Process.

When confronted with a situation that is challenging, weigh your options and proceed with the best course of action, whatever that might be. Sometimes it's just taking your medicine, chipping out into the fairway, and proceeding from there. My college golf coach used to tell me, "To make one mistake is human, but to make two in a row is just plain stupid". Nothing would upset him more than if one of his players hit a ball into the trees and then attempted some 1000-to-1 shot through the trees trying to reach the green, then having it hit the tree and drop down into an even worse position. By the way, that was usually me who tried the impossible shot. I was a very stubborn learner. One time in a college tournament I drove it into the trees. With my coach standing ten feet away from me, I was looking through a hole in the trees the size of a basketball. I was going to try this crazy shot, when I looked over at my coach and saw him giving me a look that would kill a small animal. I thought, "Ok, maybe this one time I'll chip out and play for par".

A funny thing happened. I chipped out, hit my 150 yard shot to about a foot away from the hole and made par. I swear the next twenty times I hit the ball into the same situation, I chipped out into the fairway and made par. Nothing can energize a round of golf more than to proceed correctly and be rewarded for it.

Conversely, trying the incredibly risky shot and not pulling it off and making a double bogey or worse, can be very deflating to your psyche and can make it a difficult event to recover from.

Now, I'm not saying never take chances. Just make sure you've thought all possibilities through and you're willing to accept the consequences for whichever choice you make, whatever they might be.

KNOW YOUR LIMITATIONS, THEN PUSH THEM

Knowing your limitations is crucial to success on the golf course, but there is a gray area in this concept. It's easy to know obvious limitations, such as how far you can physically carry a 3 wood. If you can hit a 3 wood no farther than 250 yards in the air, and you have 260 yards to carry a water hazard, it's obvious that you lay up. Some areas of limitations are not so obvious.

Limitations are closely related to beliefs. There is a saying, "If you believe it, you can achieve it", but I would also take into account the saying, "Honesty is the best policy". You should definitely have a strong belief in your abilities but you have to make an honest assessment of what exactly are those abilities. This knowledge is critical to successful shot making. For example, if you know that a high draw is your weakness, why would you try to hit it, even if that would be the best play to attack a certain hole location. I would recommend going to your strength, whatever that might be, and be patient that the next opportunity will be better suited to fit that strength.

This is where pushing your limits comes into play. If you struggle with a high draw, then get to the range with your instructor and hit balls daily to try to incorporate that shot into your game. It is extremely important that you have as many shots in your bag as possible. There are a lot of different shots required to play this game at the highest level, so why wouldn't you want to learn every single one of them. Until you do though, stick with your strength, be patient, and trust that whatever you try to do is what's going to work best for you. And always proceed with confidence.

THERE IS NO SUCH THING AS LUCK

I want to discuss what seems to be one of my most controversial topics, the subject of "luck". I have always had the same belief on the subject of luck and for the past 30 years, I've had more heated discussions about luck than anything else.

Here it is in a nutshell: There is no such thing as luck. Why do I believe this? First and most importantly, if you believe in luck, then you have to believe in both kinds, good and bad. There can't be good luck without bad luck. Remember, it's best to stay away from judgments and there are no stronger judgments than our belief in what is good or bad luck.

A very good friend of mine, whom I've played golf with for many years, claims in almost every round that he is *The Absolutely Unluckiest Golfer in the World!* Could you possibly think of a more negative thing to believe? I have tried to explain to him how destructive that line of thinking can be, but he wants no part of that logic. He seems content in his misery and almost uses it as a crutch. He also hasn't improved one bit in the 20 years I've golfed with him. That might be a coincidence but I doubt it.

My theory on luck is basically that it is nothing more than chance or randomness, or the laws of physics in action. Things happen for easily explainable reasons. If you hit a round ball against a tree and the ball bounces out of bounds instead of in the middle of the fairway, it's not bad luck, it's the law of physics. I recommend hitting it in the fairway.

But what if you hit it in the fairway and the ball ends up in a divot? Again, things happen. A ball has to come to rest somewhere and there are divots throughout every golf course, therefore eventually a ball will come to rest in a divot. Call it randomness or chance, better still, don't judge it all. Use it as another opportunity for greatness.

To call it bad luck is to already set yourself up for failure. Negative thoughts rarely, if ever lead to successful outcomes. To call any given situation *bad luck,* is to begin that situation with a negative thought.

I always hear "I'd rather be lucky than good". Maybe that would be true if;

A) There was such a thing as luck, and

B) If it were to happen in only one given situation and never happen like that again.

I would always rather be good than lucky, because let's face it, if you're good you don't really need to be lucky. Gary Player used to say "The harder I work, the luckier I get". What that really means is, there is no such thing as luck, we make ourselves better through hard work, not some magical concept.

Another thing about the concept of luck is that it can take your power away. I would hate to think that I worked harder and was far more talented than another player but because he was *luckier* than I, he would have the upper hand in a match. I put countless hours into the improvement of my game, so there is no way I'm going to give up the power of that *real* skill and belief in those skills, for some mythical power beyond my control.

There is an age old Chinese proverb about a rancher.

One day his prize horse escapes from the stable, and the villagers say " what bad luck that your horse is gone". The rancher says "That's neither good luck nor bad luck, just something that happened". The next day the horse returned, followed by ten more wild horses. The villagers say "what good luck that your horse returned and brought ten new horses with him". The rancher says "That's neither good luck nor bad luck, just something that happened". The rancher's son gets on one of the new horses to break him and gets thrown off and breaks his arm, and the villagers say "what bad luck that your son broke his arm". Again he says " Neither good nor bad luck, Just something that happened." The next week a warlord from a neighboring village comes to take all able-bodied young men to go off to fight a great battle where most all will surely be killed and the villagers say "What good luck that your son broke his arm and can't go off to fight in a battle that he might be killed in"...and so on.

The moral of the story is, Things happen! We rarely if ever know why, and I would say, it's really not necessary that we do know why. Things happen, so deal with it in the most positive way and move forward. Constantly wondering why things happen to us will usually lead to a "Woe, woe is me!" mentality and feeling sorry for yourself is negativity in its saddest form.

Greg Norman felt he was jinxed, but he didn't play well enough in the stretch to put the tournament away. This *allowed* his competitors the opportunity hang around long enough to chip in to beat him.

ACCEPT RESPONSIBILITY AND SUPERSTITIONS WILL BE UNNECESSARY

Similar to my beliefs on luck, are my beliefs of superstitions. Most everyone has at least one superstition that they use on a daily basis, but it seems that athletes are the most superstitious of all people. And golfers are probably the most superstitious of all athletes.

In 30 years of competitive golf I could list a thousand different superstitions used by hundreds of different golfers. Anything from their lucky ball marker to the way they mark their golf ball to their hat, socks, route to the course, breakfast before the round, etc. etc. etc.!

Silly waste of time if you ask me. Eventually, we all give up our special baby blanket. Sometimes security itself is a false sense of security! Again, your power is hard earned, so why would you want to give any of it up to an outside agent, such as a lucky ball marker? That ball marker had nothing to do with whether you made or missed a given putt. You did. And if you lost the lucky marker, does that mean you won't ever make another putt?

No matter what happens, always accept responsibility for every action and you will keep your power. This is an important concept. If we can truly accept responsibility for every action, we will never be robbed of our power. This is another debate I have with colleagues: "What if someone makes a noise or moves in my backswing? How is that my responsibility?"

First, you chose to be in that place at that time and you know that there is a possibility that these things could happen, so it's best to be prepared for anything.

Second, If your focus is what it should be, you won't hear or see any distractions. Don't allow anyone or anything to take away your power or you might find that either, everything will start to bother you or your opponents will see this as a weakness and use it against you.

Have you ever been so focused in a round of golf that a siren went off in your backswing and you didn't even hear it? This usually only happens when you're playing really well. Why are you playing so well? Because you are so focused that you are completely unaware of loud noises, unexpected movements, good or bad luck, your superstitions, or any other external or internal disturbances.

With the acceptance of responsibility comes a loss of blame. Many golfers love the blame game. It's so much easier to simply blame someone or something for your shortcomings, but it takes a strong will and true belief in one's abilities to accept responsibility for every action. If you can make that acceptance you will find an unlimited power you never knew you possessed. If there is nothing that can disturb you, or nothing you give your power to, you can play golf (or live your life) at maximum strength. You will be 100% ready to conquer any challenge before you. Ever wondered why you feel so tired at times? I'll bet if you think back on your day or week, you'll discover that you've spent so much wasted time giving away your power and usually to people or things that don't nearly deserve it. Mental exhaustion can be much more draining than physical exhaustion.

The most common ways of giving up your power is by being negative, complaining, blaming, feeling sorry for yourself, making pointless judgments, being impatient, getting angry, etc.

Avoid these emotional land mines and the quest for *full positive power* will be so much easier to achieve. A golfer with full physical and mental power is a formidable opponent.

Getting back to superstitions, I need to clarify that I do believe that rituals are important. Some rituals border on superstition and here's an example. I marked my golfball with a happy face (a dot on either side of the number and a smile under the number) for every round of golf I played as a professional after the day my daughter was born. It was a constant reminder of what brought me the most happiness in my life and a way of keeping her with me when I was away from her.

This wasn't a superstition, it was a ritual. It was a small step in the preparation of my round. It always brought a smile to my face and made me think of positive things before I hit my first shot of the day. In no way did I feel that if I didn't do this I would have bad luck or even that by marking my ball this way that it would make me play better. It was just a positive part of my repetitive pre-round ritual. Remember, repetition is the key to success in golf.

THE ILLUSION OF CONTROL

What can we actually control? I think you would be surprised to know that there are very few, if any, things that we can actually *control.* I suppose we can control where we are at any given moment and there might even be thoughts that we can control, but beyond that we are left to whims of the universe. Sure we could have an argument about the semantics of what control really is but I think that would miss the greater point, and here it is: Control is an illusion. The sooner we accept that philosophy, the easier our lives will flow. Let's look at some examples of what I mean. Once you hit a golf ball, do you really have any control over where that ball will end up? Nope. Granted, if we are fully prepared, go through the proper Process, select the correct club, and make a good swing, our chances of success greatly increase. But I've hit numerous shots that have it the pin and ricocheted into a water hazard or the sand. I thought I had control, but was taught a lesson on how the game really works.
You do your best, hope for the best result, but accept whatever happens. That's why acceptance is so much more powerful than control.
Some say that they have control over their thoughts but even that can be false. How many times has your subconscious mind screamed "Don't hit it left" in your downswing and it forced you to either hit the

shot left or you blow the ball way right. If you really had control over your thoughts that would never happen.

Why are people such control freaks? Because it can be terrifying to think that we have no control over anything. It's really a rare and courageous person that is comfortable floating through life carefree, willing to accept whatever comes his or her way. "Maybe if I can control this situation, it will go the way I want" is what most people believe. The disappointment is only magnified when things don't work out the way we planned.

How does letting go and accepting whatever happens help me on the golf course? This is a great question. The answer is that control is very closely related to expectations, and expectations are future or results-oriented thinking. Whenever we think of the results, we are not in the moment and our play can only suffer.

In college, I was in the middle of many rounds where I found myself a few shots under par. I would think, "If I can just par the last few holes I'll shoot 68 or 69" and sounded so much better than a score in the 70's. It was that kind of out-of-the-moment thinking that would inevitably lead to bogeys and disappointment.

What I learned from that way of thinking was;

A) Whenever I am not in the moment, I can't put my full attention and focus on the task at hand

B) Even if I did par the last few holes, someone else was making birdies and I would get passed by more aggressive players, and

C) Score is inconsequential. Only giving your best possible effort on every shot is what is truly important.

If we have no expectations and let go of our desire to control the situation, all things are possible. There is an amazing freedom in letting go.
Years ago I was going to play a tournament with a good friend and a great golfer, and we had just finished our bucket of balls on the range before teeing off. I happened to notice that he wasn't hitting the ball very well. We finished the warm up session at the same time and headed for the first tee. I ask him how he hit it (knowing the answer, but wanting to know what he thought) and he said "Worst I've hit it in months!". Then he said something that profoundly affected me, "I absolutely love it when that happens!" I asked him to explain. "All things are possible today," he said. He meant it in a purely positive way. He truly accepted not knowing where

the ball was going. He believed that it made him focus much more intensely.

Until I heard him say that, I had no idea just how much I needed to feel that sense of control before I played, not realizing how many expectations I was putting on myself before the round had even begun. If I hit it poorly in warm ups, I almost expected to carry that with me on the course and would play poorly. If I hit it really well in warm ups, I expected to play great but that didn't always happen, and when it didn't, I'd be even more disappointed.

Once I learned to accept that things happen beyond my control, I could stay with the Process, overcome any perceived problems, and more importantly my golf improved overnight. Also, once I learned to let go, I discovered that I was much less fatigued after the round. It is exhausting trying to hang on to the perception of control. It's nothing but wasted energy.

Chapter 3

FOCUS:
The Backbone of the Process

Here is where we get to the core of the Process. Focus is the common denominator that binds all great players. It is impossible to achieve greatness in anything without intense focus. The most glaring example of the power of *focus* in golf is Tiger Woods. In my long career in golf, I competed against, worked with, or observed thousands of players but I never saw anyone with the unrelenting pinpoint focus possessed by Tiger. He has an uncommon and unmatched ability to block out everything, stay only in the moment, and concentrate solely on the task at hand. It doesn't matter whether he was stroking a putt on the practice green or stroking a putt on the 72nd hole to win the US Open, he always brings the same intense focus. Sure he is exceptionally gifted with physical talent but it's the way he can focus unlike anyone else that makes him arguably the greatest player of all time.

As a youth his father would throw keys at him in his backswing or do other distracting things just to teach him the importance of focus and concentration. He still loses his cool when a photographer snaps a camera in his backswing or even when he hits a bad shot but he has the unique ability to let those feelings go and get right back in the moment as if the thing that just set him off never happened.

If I were working with Tiger, I would teach him not to let those things set him off in the first place. But Tiger has such a fierce competitive nature, I think he would feel (incorrectly I believe) that it would take away his fierce competitive edge. Hard to argue with his results though.

There might not ever be another Tiger Woods. There are very few people in the whole world who can swing a club the way he does but there is nothing stopping any us from having his focus. In this chapter I will discuss what it takes to learn the proper techniques of pin point focus.

Maybe first I should explain what is *Pin Point Focus*. The most important thing in golf is your target. Sometimes your target is a tree in the distance, a point 15 feet right of the hole, a spot on the green you want your chip shot to land on or the line to the hole. Whatever your target might be, there is a necessity to have pin point focus on it.

Let's set up a common scenario. Your ball lies nicely in the middle of the 18th fairway 180 yards from a green which is surrounded by sand. You have a one shot lead in a big tournament. The galleries are excited and there are distractions everywhere. At stake is a lot of money, a nice trophy, an exemption to play in the majors, a two year exemption for continuing status on the PGA Tour, etc.

Here's what should happen in that scenario. Go through your entire routine, focus only on your target, and after assuring yourself that you're ready to go, pull the trigger with confidence.

Here's what happens more often than not. We begin with laser pin point focus on our target, then we forget about going through the pre-shot routine that we work on every day. We get tight and start thinking about all the things that inevitably remove us from our target. "I need this money!", "I hope I don't choke in front of all these people!", "I really want to play in the Masters!" are some of the ridiculous but understandable thoughts that can enter the mind in stressful situations.

With every negative thought or every venture into the past or the future, the scope of vision widens. Soon instead of pin point focus, we have a broad field of vision. The wider the field of vision the greater our chances of failure. Conversely, the narrower the field of vision the greater the chances of success. Ideally, a tunnel vision-like focus produces the best results. The ability to block out all distractions and negative thoughts is the difference between an average and an exceptional player. Think of the shots you hit playing with your friends with nothing on the line. Think how relatively free and relaxed you are. Without consequences, you hit wonderfully easy feeling shots just as you intended. Why is it so easy? Because there aren't the distractions or expectations seeping into your head. It makes it easier to have that pin point focus. Well, with the proper practice and training of *The Process*, you will be able to do this no matter how big the situation might be.

5 SENSE IMAGERY

Let's jump right in with the most complex, probably most misunderstood and under used tool in a golfer's game, *imagination*. Many good players use some form of visualization during a round of golf. There is no doubt that visualizing a shot before you hit it can greatly intensify your focus and aid in the successful completion of any given shot. The problem is most players don't have a real grasp of why or how to do this properly. It takes discipline and a lot of hard work to train your mind to use it effectively and consistently.

Some peoples imagination can cause them problems. For example, my daughter used to see monsters under her bed before going to sleep and it kept her up nights. Some golfers imaginations causes them to see horrible outcomes before they even hit the shot. Imagination can be the most useful tool in a golfers game but if used improperly it can have devastating consequences. This is why it's so important to be able to train your mind to be strong and function properly. It is really only in that way that we can use our imagination as a powerful positive tool .

Young players aspiring for the PGA Tour would often ask me "What is the single thing I can do to make me a better player?". I always tell them the same thing, *start reading.* Reading is like jogging for your brain. Your brain is just like a muscle and needs constant conditioning to operate at peak form.

My mother read over 5,000 books in her life. I almost never saw her watch TV. She was one of the most intelligent person's I ever knew. I on the other hand was never a big reader. I read basically just to get my college degree. I would read an occasional novel in my free time but I was too enamored with athletics to sit still for any given period of time. When I started to play golf professionally, I discovered that there was a lot of travel and down time, so I began to read just to pass the time. At first it was fiction and then I graduated to deeper more complex spiritual journey type books. The more complex the better for the brain. Simple, less complex books are like running on a treadmill, in that reading them will help you get fit. But deep complex reading is like cross training for your brain because it involves the use of your imagination and intellect to stay focused.

I began by reading for 15 minutes and I would wake up drooling with my face stuck to the book. Then I could read for about 15 minutes without falling asleep. There were times when I would read for a set period of time and when I would stop, I couldn't remember anything about what I just read. Soon though, I could read for an hour without falling asleep. Eventually I could read for an hour with total comprehension. It took me about four months of at least one hour a day of reading to get to that level. After about a year of reading every day, I could read without fatigue for hours on end. During one particular tournament in Palm Springs, I stayed alone at a friend's house. I wanted to rest my body the day before the tourney, so I began to read a new book. It was a Sci-Fi cult classic novel called "Stranger in a Strange Land". The book was very complex, fascinating, and probably about 450 pages long. I laid out by the pool all day and finished the book in one sitting, something I had never done in my life. Not only did I finish the book but I had full comprehension and was totally immersed in the story.

My mind was never stronger than at that moment in my life. I easily won that two day tournament and had never used my 5 Sense Imagery technique with such intensity.

What is 5 Sense Imagery?

5 Sense Imagery is just what it sounds like, the use of all five of your senses to imagine the shot you are about to play. That's right, sight, sound, feel, smell, and yes even taste. I know what you're thinking, "How can I taste a cut 5 iron shot over a water hazard?" Why you should taste that shot is more important than how to taste it but I'll explain both. It's important to add all senses to your pre-shot routine because your mind can only handle so many thoughts at one time. If you are thinking about the taste of the gum you are chewing, your mind has just a little less space for a negative thought to enter. Like I said, most golfers have dabbled in the use of visualization in their pre-shot routines and that's a good thing. Once you learn how to incorporate all your senses, you'll find out something amazing. The intensity of your focus will increase 500%.

Here is a technique you can use to help strengthen your 5 Sense Imagery.

At the driving range, physically hit golf shots while chewing mint gum and noticing the certain smell of the pine trees or nearby flowers or the cut grass. Then step back and imagine yourself standing in front of *you* hitting shots. In your mind's eye, see yourself swinging the club. Feel your body in motion and the club striking the ball. Hear the sound it makes when you contact the ball solidly. Imagine the taste of the gum and the smell of pine. Do this over and over again and eventually you will strengthen your imagination and your mind. It takes a little work and some time but when you can do this consistently, you will find that in the most stressful situations that your pre-shot routine and focus will be so strong that sirens could go off in your backswing and you wouldn't even notice.

If you can integrate 5 Sense Imagery into your game, you'll have accomplished two crucial things. First, you will know that your mental approach is strong and that all the hard work you put into strengthening your mind has paid off. Nothing could be more rewarding for your psyche or for your confidence then to see the fruits of your hard work come to fruition.

Second, you'll discover that the concentration required to use your imagination at that level will nearly eliminate the entrance of negative thoughts or distractions into your head. You will be so focused on the task at hand, that even the most stressful situations will seem routine.

It's very important that you put the 5 Sense Imagery into every shot you hit, whether it be in practice or tournament play. In very stressful situations, most golfers are thrown off their rhythm, easily distracted, get tight in their muscles, and their adrenaline flows.

This is when the pre-shot routine that you work on every day in play or practice is so important. Bad thoughts can easily invade your mind in these stressful times, so the more positive thoughts (like imagining a perfect shot) you can put in your head, the better.

Remember, any golfer can produce an entire pre-shot routine in a matter of seconds, including; strategy assessment and club selection, shot rehearsal, 5 Sense Imagery, and pulling the trigger only when ready.

Here is another exercise you can try to assist you in sharpening your imagination. When you get in bed before you go to sleep, turn off all electronic devices and meditatively quiet your mind. Now, start to play golf holes in you head. Stand behind each shot and imagine the entire hole. See the trees, the fairway, and your target in the distance. Again, imagine the smells of pine and the taste of the gum you're chewing. Feel yourself addressing the ball and the movements your body makes. Hear the sound made as the clubhead makes contact with the ball. Repeat again and again. It is an exhaustive exercise and you'll find yourself falling asleep rather quickly at first try. Think of preparing for a marathon. The first day of road work you would probably be exhausted after a mile or so. Eventually though, with enough training you could work up to conditioning your body to run a full marathon. Exercising your mind works nearly the same way.

In my head while lying in bed, I would play every hole of the course I was going to play the next day in a tournament. Sometimes it would take up to two hours but the next day I had a very good idea of what I wanted to do on every hole. I always felt ready to play and prepared to deal with the unexpected, because in my mind, I had already played the holes successfully.

Conscious vs. Subconscious

To put it simply, the conscious mind powers our thoughts and the subconscious mind powers our beliefs. You can think or say whatever you want but what you believe in the deepest regions of you psyche is what will most likely determine the outcome of any venture.

With a 10 foot putt to win the tournament, you can tell yourself as sternly as possible that you are going to make this putt but if deep down inside you don't really believe in yourself, it's most likely not going to happen. Often this failure under pressure is known as *Choking*. I believe that the term "choking" is overused and misused. Just because you miss a 3 foot putt to win, that doesn't necessarily mean choking was the cause. If you went through your Process properly and had nothing but positive thoughts, these putts can still be missed. That's just a part of the game.

Choking is basically letting fear determine the outcome. If you proceed with a shot, doing everything required to be successful and you still fail, that is not a choke. But if you attempt to hit a shot knowing that you're not ready or because the situation is just too big for you or that you have a fear of any number of things, failure is the most likely outcome.

The proper method is to train your mind to believe that no matter what the situation is, you have a belief system in place to carry you through. How to do this isn't as easy as you might think.

Your subconscious is the total sum of all the thoughts you have ever had in your life. Throughout this enormous mass of accumulated information, there is formed a general conception of what you think of yourself. If you have spent your life complaining, whining, blaming others for your problems, and living a life of negative thinking and actions, deep down in your subconscious there would be little confidence or any real self belief. But it is never too late to change if you have a real desire to do so. You just have to want to change. Remember, we have spent a lifetime developing our character and personality, so don't think that years of negative input in your subconscious will easily be replaced with positive thoughts. It requires a lot of work but if you're willing to put in the time, the change will astonish you.

Let's begin RIGHT NOW! If you want to make a change in your life, the best time to do it is now, not tomorrow or next week.

It can be amazing to see just how negative your thinking can be when you try to go a whole day without a negative thought. Just try to do it for five minutes! It's not easy. In fact, 15 years ago when I tried to make this change, it took me about two years of daily mental training to see real consistent positive results. But what results they were! I would never want to go back to the way I used to think, and yet, I spent 30 plus years developing that personality. Every once in a while though, a negative thought pops into my head from my old personality. It's a constant struggle but a battle that must be won to find success with any endeavor. That old negative personality is like a powerful spring that you have to keep your hand on all the times. If you take your hand off for a moment, up pops that spring and the negative thoughts it represents. The longer you can keep your hand on the spring, the less power it has. Eventually, when enough time and training has been put into creating your new more positive attitude and character, it will be much easier to minimize that old negative character.

Let's examine some examples of what is the difference between the conscious and subconscious mind. Let's go back to that 10 foot put to win a tournament. Once you've gone through your pre-shot routine and stand over the ball, this is when you want outer and inner thoughts to coincide. You can tell yourself until your blue in the face that you are going to make this putt (and that is exactly what you should do) but if deep down inside you don't really believe it, it's probably not going to happen, and here is why. Your conscious mind determines the success of the backswing and your subconscious determines the success of the approach into and through the ball.

What exactly does that mean? Back to the 10 foot putt. You go through all of the thoughts required to make yourself take that putter back steady, smooth, and on plane. Once that club begins it's approach into the ball, your conscious mind is done with it's work and the subconscious takes over *whether you want it to or not*. It could be screaming at you and you'll only know it by the result of the stroke. Fears infest your mind and they manifest themselves in the subconscious thought process. What this means is that your mind must be free of fears and negative thoughts before you hit any shot to insure a positive result. If your thoughts are not pure, "Don't pull it!" or "Don't hit it too hard!" will pop into your head seemingly from nowhere and failure is inevitable.

I used to employ tricks to help me through those difficult moments. I would say to myself as I was in the process of stroking a putt, "Straight back, straight through" or "One, Two, and through". What this would do is keep my mind on a simple rhythmic phrase so I wouldn't have a negative thought pop into my head in the follow through. I learned that it was much better to remove those negative thoughts altogether, then to try to constantly *trick* myself. In this way, I can proceed with the knowledge that I've done everything I could have done to prepare myself for this situation. I won't have to worry about what the consequences of my actions will be. I can be positive and confident with the notion that I'm ready to win and that I'm willing to accept whatever comes with the impending results.

When the subconscious is clear, confident, and fearless, the approach into and through the ball will be flowing and effortless. The results will undoubtedly be more successful, even when goals aren't met. Don't let the fact that the ball didn't go into the hole determine whether you succeeded or not. Know that if you went through the Process exactly the way you are supposed to and committed fully to doing the best you could in that moment, you were very successful no matter the result.

In the long run, your game will greatly improve if you're doing the Process properly. Sometimes the ball goes in and sometimes it doesn't but it will certainly go in the hole much more if the Process is followed correctly and continuously.

THE POWER OF THE PRESENT

Almost everyone has heard the expression, "The past is history, the future is a mystery, and the present is a gift, that's why it's called *the present!*", but few people understand the awesome power of staying in the present.

Most of us live our lives everywhere but the here and now. We are constantly thinking about what is ahead of us or what has just happened to us, but it's in *this moment* which is the only place where we can truly *live*.

The irony of this simple fact is that staying in the moment is probably the most difficult thing that we can do. The untrained mind sees and hears distractions at every turn. How many times have you been reading a book or listening to someone and a few moments go by and you realize that you didn't comprehend a thing. You were many miles away, thinking about something completely unrelated to your book or conversation. *In fact, I'm confident that each time you read this book, you will pick up something new and your understanding of the Process will increase as your mind gets stronger.*

Our minds wander when they are weak and untrained. A trained mind finds clarity and tranquility in even the most stressful situations. Though the brain is the most complex organism in the universe, with the ability to store billions of bits of information, it still works best with simple single-minded *in the moment* focus.

I can actually hold three conversations, be reading, and watch tv all at the same time but it usually gets me into trouble because I always miss the most important facts. Imagine listening to three different songs all playing loudly at the same time. Individually, they all might sound beautiful but together they are a confusing, distracting mess.

In stressful (or even mundane) situations, if there are numerous thoughts racing through our mind, the most important fact is usually missed.

A golf example: You're standing on the tee of the 72nd hole with a one shot lead. Trouble is everywhere and yesterday you made double bogey on the hole. The tournament is on the line, you need the money, you want your name on the trophy, a while back you failed in the same situation or you're fighting your swing, are just some of the thoughts racing through your head.

I could go on and on but if you've played the game at all, you know exactly what I'm talking about. If your mind is thinking about all of these things at once, it sounds like three songs playing loudly in your head. It sets up for an improbable chance at success when you're heart is racing and your mind is confused and rattled. The trained mind is prepared for the situation and is calm. It focuses on one *in the moment* thought, unlike the pandemonium going on in the mind of the untrained. You can look at the two players, one untrained and one trained, and it's apparent who's in a better place to succeed in that situation.

The trained mind is relaxed but aware. It has the understanding that a certain calmness and composure are required to proceed with focus and confidence.

The untrained mind is rattled, distracted, out of sync, and uncomfortable with the situation at hand and not focusing on the moment.

How do we learn to stay in the moment? Like I said, it's difficult. It works best with a strong mind and strong body. We have to train it for these very situations. Most of us can compete when things are going our way or the situation isn't too big. It's when times get stressful that the best trained minds surpass the rest.

In this book, I'll go over the some keys to meditation, self-hypnosis, and some focus exercises that will give you a good foundation of what to practice with your mental training.

Getting back to the 72nd hole with the tourney on the line, here is what the proper thought process should go like, to best stay in the moment.

1) Assess the physical. What are the obstacles of the hole, where is the best place to hit the ball, and what is the best club to hit for proper ball placement.

2) Once you've assessed your physical situation, it's time for your mental training to kick in. Take a few deep cleansing breaths. Feel the anxiety leaving your body with every breath. Your mind is calming down and your heart rate is slowing. It's very important that things appear to be moving slowly. Don't proceed until you feel ready and confident.

3) Focus in on the target to aim your shot at it with tunnel vision, then tell yourself "I will hit this shot right at that target".

4) Go through your pre-shot routine just as you do with every single shot you hit, again with tunnel vision focus on your target.

5) Ask yourself if you are ready to hit this shot, when and only when the answer is "Yes I am", then you proceed with the shot.

Here are some things that should already be built into your subconscious through the training learned in this book.

1) No matter what the result of the shot is, you are willing to accept it. Whether it be perceived as good or bad.

2) In the grand scheme of things, is this shot really going to change the world? Meaning, though your situation might seem so to you at the time, actually the suffering in Darfur or the plight of the homeless or a million other things that affect the human race, are probably more important. Putting things in the proper perspective, can help you understand what is truly important and help alleviate some of the pressure we all build up in our minds.

3) Golf is supposed to be fun! Sometimes the pressure built up in our minds can be crushing, uncomfortable, and even mentally and physically painful. Try to remember in difficult times, this is just a game and we play it because it's fun. Again, it's about proper perspective, and remember, it's ok to smile.

4) Through this training, a true sense of self will be developed. You should be loving, understanding, patient, and have a real belief that you are going to

be successful at whatever you do. There is nothing stronger than a person who truly has belief in themselves.

With the proper training, a lot of work and practice, all of these requirements can be acquired by anyone. I know we look at people we admire and think, "That could never be me" but I'm telling you it can be you. We are all special in some way or another. Most are all born pretty much the same. It's just that those exceptional few who rise to the top, are the ones that seem willing to put in the extra work, have the proper guidance, and believe in what they are doing. It's never too late to start and never too late to make a change in our lives that make us not just better golfers, but more complete human beings.

SELF TALK

From my earliest childhood memories of the way my father would speak to me, I remember that he was so careful about the words he used and the words he would allow me to use. I learned what the word *semantics* meant long before any of my friends. Having a father with a Ph.D in Psychology and a mother with a Master's in Linguistics gave me a head start on my vocabulary and a full understanding of the power of words.

My mother taught me how to read before I was in kindergarten and both my parents gave me the green light to ask them any question, no matter how uncomfortable it made them feel. This taught me to question everything, because I just loved the acquisition of knowledge.

I became a skeptic at an early age. I also became a very good listener. I didn't just hear the words, I listened for their true deeper meaning. Listening intently to others made me understand, that what a person says wasn't as important as their actions. But I more importantly learned that if you really listen to what a person is saying, what they say can tell you a lot about what they think of themselves. *Self talk* is the outward expression of what we think of ourselves. How many times have you hit a poor shot and in utter frustration yelled out loud for everyone to hear..."YOU IDIOT! How could you hit such a stupid shot!"? At first glance you would obviously think, there goes someone who isn't too happy with themselves. You think it's something they might say just in the heat of the moment but this is the kind of self talk that is festering deep in the subconscious at all times. Depending on what you really feel about yourself, there is often a frequent audible monologue representing your true feelings.

Sadly, most self talk is negative. Rarely do you hear anyone patting themselves on the back after a good shot for fear of being considered arrogant but you'll hear all kinds of negative dialogue throughout a round of golf. Being that this inner dialogue becomes outward mostly when the judgments of your performance are perceived to be negative, one would have to assume there is a deep seeded insecurity. It's at this time that a serious assessment of the self talk and the cause of these insecurities needs to be addressed immediately.

By following *The Process* and practicing it regularly, you will begin to see and feel a positive change in your attitude. Once your attitude changes in a more positive direction, you will begin to see and hear a noticeable change in your actions and words. You'll be kinder to yourself and others will notice the change in your personality. This to will add to your self confidence. Confidence breeds confidence and it all begins with the way you treat yourself. You'll also notice that people will treat you more positively when you treat yourself better.

It's important to note that sometimes no matter what you do, no matter how correctly you follow the appropriate plan, things just don't go the way you want.

I had a student of mine once tell me after a difficult round, "I was as positive as I could have been and everything still went to shit!". I smiled and asked him if he had fun. He said emphatically "NO". I said "Well then I don't think you were being as positive as you could be". He then smiled and agreed with me. The next day, he honestly used the Process and shot 66. After that round he told me that he realized just how bad his self talk was the previous day and how much fun he had on this day. Remember what I always write in this book, "Golf Is a marathon, not a sprint". Some days are good and some days are perceived as not so good. The important point to note is that if you stick with the Process, in the long run, the results will *always* be so much better. Maybe not better in this one particular moment but certainly for the future. Another thing I like to say is, "We take care of our future in the present".

So always talk nicely to yourself, because even if things don't seem to be working out in this moment, they will if you keep positive and trust the path you are on. This will lead you to the goals and desires you have set for yourself.

SELF-HYPNOSIS AND MEDITATION

Self-hypnosis and meditation are two concepts that for the most part go unused by even the most accomplished golfer or anyone else for that matter. I know just the thought of them conjure up images of long haired hippie types in tie dyed t-shirts, chanting in beaded rooms which reek of incense. Or some shady character with a handlebar mustache waving a pocket watch back and forth before your eyes and saying "Your getting very sleepy" in a creepy voice. Well, I'm here to tell you that when used correctly, they can be the tools that make the difference between achieving great accomplishments and a constant struggle with mediocrity.

Many of the situations I set up for you in this book, deal with the most stressful moments in any given round. I do this to accentuate the point but the truth is, there are very few individuals who even put themselves in these situation in the first place.

How do we even get to the point of having a putt to win a tournament? The easy answer is lots of hard work and fortunate circumstances. I believe that those who (with all things being relatively equal) find themselves in these amazing situations are the ones who have the ability to alter their tension, emotions, heart rate, and thoughts.

There are a handful of individuals who can do this naturally, with almost a given ability to maintain a calmness under pressure, but they are indeed a rare breed. I would say that they learned something similar to meditation at some point in their life which has subconsciously slipped it's way into their everyday routines.

For those of us who, let's say aren't so fortunate, there are ways to develop that calmness.

Let's begin by defining the basic difference between the two. Self-hypnosis is a tool by which one may inject positive thoughts and ideas into their subconscious. Meditation is a tool used for relaxation and cleansing of the mind.

Both of these forms of mental training require a deep trance-like state for there to be a full effective benefit, this is why you need the proper training for them to work for you.

Whether we want to admit it or not, the one thing that usually holds us back in life is the way we think. If you're not where you want to be in your life or career, most of the time it's because you have developed a set of bad habits that establish how you proceed in any given situation.

We all suffer from our own bad habits but we don't seem to have a clear way to change them. We get into a rut and we have no idea how we got there or how to get out. Ever done something and wondered, "Why in the hell did I just do that?". You did it because you have conditioned yourself to behave the same way under certain similar situations. Like Pavlov's dogs, when we hear a bell ring, we salivate.

Our habits and rituals develop throughout our lives, because they usually bring us comfort, even when pain is the outcome. A classic example is the person who is commitment phobic or insecure in a relationship. They do everything they can to sabotage the relationship so it won't hurt so bad when the person (whom they believe will inevitably leave them anyway) ends the relationship. It becomes more comfortable destroying what could have been a great thing, then to fight for the one's they love and risk being crushed later on down the road.

The only successful way to rid ourselves of these bad habits is to train ourselves to believe a different way. "The definition of insanity they say, is to do the same thing every time and expect a different result." Yet who among us makes a mistake only once? We need to break the endless cycle of making the same mistakes over and over again, and the best way to do that is through self-hypnosis and meditation.

Let's begin with Self-hypnosis. This can be done in a seated position but is best when lying down in a quiet dimly lit place with all electronic devices turned off as to not be interrupted. It's very important that you set aside about fifteen to thirty minutes where nothing or no one can disturb you. It takes a while to get yourself in the right place, so you don't want that state of mind to be broken.

Once you are ready to begin, you start with about ten deep slow breaths. Inhale slowly and exhale slowly. With each breath, you feel the tension being pushed out of your body through your fingers and toes. Once you've repeated ten breaths and you feel relaxed (if more breaths are required for a state of relaxation, then keep doing deep breathing until you feel ready to proceed) you are now ready to begin your *journey*.

I'll describe my journey, but it's best if you create your own. I begin by walking down a dimly lit long hallway until I reach a flight of descending stairs (remember to keep taking long deep cleansing breaths throughout your session). With each step down the stairs I feel a deeper sense of relaxation. Near the bottom of the long stairway, I can see a little more light and I hear the sound of a gentle stream flowing through a cave. When I get to the bottom of the stairs, there is a platform with a padded raft waiting for me. I get on the raft, lie down, and begin to float down the gentle stream. In the distance, I can see the opening to the cave and I feel the sensation of warmth from the sun. When exiting the tunnel from within the cave, I float down stream through a beautiful forest. I feel the sun glimmering through the trees and hitting me in the face. As I continue to float down stream, I feel an amazingly powerful energy that brings a feeling of confidence and security to my psyche. I feel that I have no troubles or worries and that when I step off this raft I am new and alive, like this will be the first day of a new and positive existence. As the stream gets narrower and less flowing, the raft slows to a stop and my eyes open. I feel strong and rejuvenated, ready for whatever the moment brings me.

This journey should take at least 15 minutes but mine usually go for about thirty. Feel free to interject positive thoughts into your subconscious as you float down stream. Tell yourself what a great golfer or what a patient and forgiving person you are. The more positive reinforcement the better. This is important because even the most positive person may still have many negative thoughts floating around in their subconscious. This practice can be used to wash away the bad thoughts and replace them with good ones.

Meditation is a mind cleansing tool. It's really nothing more than a way to find peace and tranquility in our everyday hectic lives. Meditation, unlike self-hypnosis can be done in a few minutes. You can do it anywhere or anytime (though I wouldn't recommend it while driving or operating heavy machinery). I have often *Mini-meditated* before I hit a difficult golf shot or when I feel a stressful situation coming on. Like self-hypnosis, meditation begins with deep cleansing breaths. The difference is, with meditation the goal is really only to slow the heart rate and clear or calm the mind.

Continue to breathe deeply and use a sound or a chant phrase that can be used as a focus point for you to center your energy on. A deep tonal *UHMMMMMM* as you exhale is slowly repeated or a non-sensical phrase will help to deepen your focus. Center your focus on only one thing, such as a candle, flower, or the flagstick and place all your attention on it. Notice every detail of the object and burn it into your memory. Breathe deeply and again, feel all the bad energy being pushed out of your body when you exhale and all the world's positive energy being sucked into your body when you inhale. Think of your mind as a chalkboard with all the problems of your day written on it and with every cleansing breath, you erase a problem. Don't stop until you feel that all your worries have been erased and an involuntary smile comes to your face.

Again, you awake to a feeling of peaceful energy, like you are brand new and ready for the moment. Like I said, I could do this before a particularly scary tee shot or putt, in only a few moments. Instead of a candle or flower, your focus point is an image of what you want to accomplish, whether it be holing the putt or the flight of a perfectly struck tee shot. Take your deep cleansing breaths, slow your heart rate, feel a sense of relaxation flowing through your body and erase any negative thoughts from your mental chalkboard. This might take one minute or two and will leave you feeling much more relaxed and confident. The next time you watch a golf tournament on TV, look to see the players taking deep cleansing breaths before difficult shots or in stressful moments. You should see them do this quite often.

It takes a few months of consistent practice but once you are comfortable and confident that you have a grasp of your own technique, you will be amazed at how easy and necessary self-hypnosis and meditation will be.

Life can be difficult at times, whether it be brought on by external or our own internal challenges. We all need a way to navigate through, or even remove, the obstacles that are put in our paths. I believe these two simple stress management techniques can greatly assist you with your journey.

I believe that we are all born pure and with an illuminating light from within our core. As we grow older and more cynical, we begin to develop thought patterns that only assist in bringing a negative flow our way. With every negative thought or action we throw another chunk of mud on the internal light. By the time some of us are *grown-ups,* we have covered the entire ball of light with mud, so that no light shines through. It is then that all things seem dark and dire. With no light shining through, we see no hope and when there is no hope, we sometimes resort to desperate measures. We sink deeper into an abyss of negativity and self pity. It's only when we hit rock bottom that we search for an answer and help. If we give up, we fall forever into the abyss.

You don't need to let it get this bad. I may be getting away from what makes a great golfer but I believe it's better and easier to be a great golfer if you are first a happier person.

Use the practices of self-hypnosis and meditation to help wipe away all of the mud and muck that is covering your light. If you can do this, that light will help you to navigate through dark times, until the point when things won't be dark at all.

Once you begin to live your life in the light, you'll find that there really aren't any obstacles. That the things that used to be frustrating and cause worry, really aren't anything but imaginary monster's that you've built up in your mind. You won't see them as monster's anymore or even problems. They are only situations that can easily be dealt with. Besides, nothing is really a problem, only a situation. If problems are ever solved, they are only soon replaced by another problem. Better to think of them as situations, because a situation can be dealt with, never to return.

IN THE ZONE, NOT A MAGICAL PLACE

Every golfer has heard the phrase *in the zone.* It's the place where nothing seems to go wrong and it can last for a single shot or in Tiger Woods case about ten years.

The Zone is usually referred to as a magical place which only happens on rare occasions and with no rhyme or reason. It's believed that it can't be conjured up at will and that we never know when or if we'll find ourselves in it.

Often times, someone is referred to as being *unconscious* when in a zone-like state. Although *unconscious* is usually used as a derogatory term, this is not far from the truth. The way we access the zone is through our subconscious, assuming our subconscious is well trained and possessing true self belief. You can't consciously think your way into the zone. It's a bit like self-hypnosis in that you can't just say "I believe I'm going to be in the zone", you have to go through a set process and develop an internal belief system. This ability to access the *zone* may take some work.

Baseball pitchers are considered to be *in the zone* from about the fifth inning of a "no hit" bid. His teammates stay away from him and never mention the possible no hitter, as to not jinx it or to wake him from the magical zone he is in.

In golf, we see it when someone has just birdied three or four holes in a row. It's perceived as such a fragile state that the slightest distraction can *awaken* us and burst the bubble that we are enveloped within.

I discovered my theory of the zone while playing a round of golf years ago with friends. There was some gambling going on and the usual chatter and ribbing but this never concerns me. From my first swing, I had a feeling this was going to be a special day on the course. With intense focus, I hit shot after shot exactly the way I had imagined. I was oblivious to the attempts to throw me off my game and made the turn at 4 under par. After three more birdies, I was in the middle of the 16th fairway and had just hit another shot next to the flagstick. I picked up my bag and started walking to the green when I thought I had heard a loud whistle. Still walking, I heard it again. I turned around to see the other four member of my group with their hands out yelling for me to get out of the way. It was at that moment that I realized how deeply *in the zone* I was. I didn't even realize that I was playing with anyone. I was so focused on what I was doing that I was truly in my own world. No sounds or distraction. Nothing but tunnel vision focus. Their whistles broke me out of my trance and I missed the putt. I did finish the round with a score of 65 on a difficult golf course but I learned something that day which was much more important than my score. I learned that *The Zone* wasn't a magical place that is entered only by chance. *The Zone* is a place you can put yourself whenever you want.

All *The Zone* is really, is an intense tunnel vision focus sustained for a period of time. Nothing more. There is no magic involved, though there is a lot of work required to develop the correct Process. You must have all the tools in your bag working properly to place yourself in the zone. If you think about it logically and if you could see the situation you're in with an intense positive focus, how could anything deny you from living in the zone? Sure things can be perceived as going wrong to casual observers but if you truly stay with your Process you won't even notice. This allows you to keep the tunnel vision focus and it's in that focus where positive things happen.

There are things that absolutely deny access to the zone. Negative thoughts, not staying in the moment, poor preparation, inconsistencies in your Process, off course distractions, and so on, will make it impossible to access the zone. Although, all these negative things will do something else, they will put you in *The Negative Zone.* This is almost never talked about but the *negative zone* is just as powerful. In fact it may be more powerful because due to human nature, the *negative zone* is so much easier to enter.

Ever have one of those days where everything just *seems* to goes wrong? That is the *negative zone*. You are so unaware of your negativity, that you (incorrectly of course) think everything seems to be against you. It can become a snow ball rolling down hill and when it gets to the point of your inability to stop it, you are fully engulfed in the *negative zone*. With a developed and strong Process put in place, you will never find yourself in the *negative zone*. This is why it's so important to practice your Process. Once you've practiced it thoroughly, you'll feel strong enough to combat the negative thoughts and you'll find it much easier to gain access to the most positive of all places...*The Zone.*

THE YIPS

This is a painful subject for most golfers, as almost everyone has experienced *the yips* at some point in their golfing career. Physically, the yips are the twitch in your hands or body that happen just before impact. It's a flinch that can drive you mad! Usually you don't even know what causes them. You figure it's just nerves but you'd be wrong. We all get nervous but most of the time we manage our nerves and proceed with successful outcomes.
The yips never bring successful results, because even when we *yip it* in the hole, we feel so

concerned that we have the yips that we have difficulty getting that thought out of our head. It's similar to the *Shanks*. The difference between the yips and the shanks is that though they can both cause mental anguish, the shanks can be fixed in one lesson from a good teaching professional. The yips, without the Process, might take some serious psychoanalysis to correct.

The yips aren't a mechanical problem, this can't be emphasized enough. It doesn't matter how mechanically perfect and flowing your putting stroke might be. The yips are something that is deeply ingrained in your psyche and need to be addressed with an honest (and sometimes painful) assessment of what is causing them. The yips are cause by fear, but what it is that you are afraid of is often difficult to pin point.

Some people are afraid of failure, some are even afraid of success. No one wants to fail, so that fear of failure can put extra pressure on you. The fear of success is a little more puzzling. With success comes attention and some people shy away from the limelight. When they find themselves as the center of attention it puts additional pressure on them through the form of expectations. It's these expectations which can bring on an uncertainty in your abilities and may in turn bring on the yips. Other fears include, financial needs, the opinions of our peers, not wanting to look foolish, attachment to the results, etc. There are many things that can cause tension and stress which affect the fluidity of our stroke or swing.

What is the cure for *the Yips*? Though there is no magic wand that can be waved, yet there are ways to remove the affliction once and for all.

You need to ask yourself what it is that you are afraid of and often the answer isn't readily apparent. If you don't search honestly for the cause of your fears, your chances of removing them are limited. Once you've determined the deep rooted cause of your fear, you can begin to minimize it's detrimental affects.

Remember, the backswing is determined by the conscious and the follow through is determined by the subconscious. If there is a fear in your subconscious it will manifest itself as a flinch just before contact. It doesn't matter how perfect your stroke or swing is, if you have doubts or fear you will flinch and even a minute flinch can cause failure in the moment.

I feel that the leading cause of the yips is *attachment to the result*. Of course you want to set goals but you don't want to get too attached to the results. For example, your goal might be to make a 20 foot putt. If you're too worried about what might happen if you don't achieve your goal, that attachment to the result will make it very difficult to successfully pull off that stroke with confidence and fluidity. It's always more important to be confident and fluid, than it is to make the putt.

Making the putt is the result and you have no control over the results. What little control we do possess is in our belief that the Process we've worked so hard to develop will work much more consistently. With real belief comes fluidity and confidence, and a detachment from the results. Think about it, if you really didn't concern yourself with the results, things would happen easily and stress free, just like when you're playing for fun with your friends. An example of this would be hitting balls on the driving range as opposed to hitting a shot in a tournament under pressure.

On the range, you're relaxed and completely unconcerned with where you ball goes because it doesn't really matter. Once you get on the course and every shot is considered *important,* tension sets in and you start to worry about where your ball will end up (the result). Detachment to the results is the key to fluidity and confidence and to removing once and for all, those dreaded yips.

IDENTIFYING NEGATIVE THOUGHTS

One thing I'm seldom asked is, "What is a negative thought?". It would almost seem to be too obvious of an answer. The funny thing is that most people have negative thoughts swimming around in their heads all day long and never know it.

When discussing what is or isn't a negative thought, we have to be a bit judgmental and it's these judgments that can often lead to more trouble. I would say though that a negative thought becomes negative only after it has been *energized*. Say you were standing on the tee and you saw water to the left of the fairway. Just to say "There is water left" isn't a negative thought, you're merely stating a fact. But to say "If I hit the ball into the water it will cost me the tournament!", then that way of thinking would give energy to the thought and make it negative. We never want to energize a negative thought because it opens the door to other negative thoughts and the next thing you know, your mind is filled with them.

Negative thoughts are like little soldiers. If you allow them into your head, they dig trenches and are extremely difficult to remove. Once they are entrenched in your head, they whistle for all there rotten little buddies to come on in and the next thing you know your head is filled with entrenched negative thoughts. Most of the time the average person walks around with a head full of negative thoughts and isn't even aware of it but it shows in their actions.

Only the most exceptionally trained mind can keep from energizing these awful thoughts. Until you have trained your mind to block them out, here are five things you can do to avoid the build up of them in your head.

1) You must understand what a negative thought is to you and not give it any energy. There is no problem with stating facts, like the fact that water is left of the fairway or that above the pin position is not the best place from which to putt. The problem comes from adding energy to these facts. When energy is added to the facts, fear, nervousness, and tension enters the equation and nothing good can ever happen.

2) Know that negative thoughts are like clouds in the sky. They often appear from nowhere and float across your *Mind's Sky*. Let them float on by and use positive thoughts to push them away. Once this negative thought has passed and a positive thought has replaced it, you can proceed with confidence because you never gave that negative thought energy and it wasn't allowed to entrench itself into your mind.

3) Positive thinking is a natural roadblock to negative thoughts. It's very difficult to think a bad thought right after you just found out you've won the lottery. Your head is filled with too many thoughts of all the great things you could do with the money.

Hopefully you're not thinking about what rotten luck it was to win all this money because now people will want to take it from you. Believe it or not, there are some people who just can't help themselves. They can find the negative in any situation. Keep your head filled with positive thoughts and you'll leave little room for the negative thoughts.

4) If you've seen the movie "Star Wars" you know what *The Force* means. The force is an energy that surrounds everything in the universe. Those who are in touch with the force can feel when there is a disturbance in it. Once you've developed a strong sense of the Process, you'll be able to sense a disturbance when a negative thought is trying to dig a trench in your mind and you'll be able to eliminate it before it's dug in.

5) Be happy! Life is good and there are a lot of other things that you could be doing that are a lot worse.

To illustrate this point, let me tell you what happened to me. In 2000 I played in the US Open at Pebble Beach. Tiger Woods won by 15 strokes but I didn't care because this was a great week for me. I soaked up every minute of it. I signed hundreds of autographs and for at least that week, I felt like one of the best players in the world. Life doesn't get much better for a professional golfer than to play in a major championship.

Little did I know that chronic bad problems would soon end the professional golfing career that I loved so much. Less then four years after my US Open experience, I would end up digging a hole covered and with dirt. I got a job in construction and started at the bottom by digging foundations for the installation of street lights. It didn't take long for me to remember just how good I had it when I was playing. It was humbling for me to come home everyday covered in dirt, back aching, and not exactly loving what I did for my new career.

I refused to let it get me down. I kept up my positive thinking and in six months, I went from a manual laborer to field supervisor. Five years later, I left the construction industry to get back to what I love and what I know the most about, Golf. I guess the moral of the story is to never take anything for granted and always enjoy what you are doing when you are doing it. It's essential to stay positive, for things will always have a better outcome.

WHAT IF THINGS GO WRONG?

Without a doubt the most commonly asked question I get from my students is "What if I follow the Process perfectly and things still go wrong?". Here is my short answer, "Accept it and move on". The difficulty for most though, is that golf is by far the most technically demanding of all sports. The complexities of the game are endless. No other sporting venture requires such demanding precision while providing a seemingly infinite amount of obstacles.

The quest for perfection is an admirable one but to expect its complete attainment is ridiculous. Yes, even when the Process is followed perfectly, things can go wrong.

I'll never forget attending a clinic put on by Gary Player when I was 13 years old. He stood in the middle of a horseshoe shaped crowd of about 300 people telling stories and demonstrating shots. The thing he said that stood out the most was when a person asked him how he handles making a double bogey.

He said "I absolutely love the adversity! If golf was that easy anyone could do it, so when things go wrong I smile and focus even harder on the next shot." Even at the age of 13, I thought that was an awesome answer. Every time I made a double bogey or worse (which sadly happened a lot in my career), Mr. Player's words ran through my head and I rarely let it affect my next shot.

Once in a two day tournament on my home course in Pasadena, California I was rolling through a great first round. I made the turn at 4 under par for a front nine of 32. I hit a drive down the middle on the 10th hole and my ball ended up in a deep divot. I looked at it as an opportunity for greatness. The second shot is over a hazard but I felt I could get enough of the ball to carry the trouble. I was wrong. The ball didn't carry far enough, landed in the hazard, and I went on to make double bogey on the hole.

My playing partner was a young pro I had played with a few times and considered a friend. Walking to the next tee he asked politely, "How do you handle that when you were playing so well?" My honest response was "Handle what?" He said "The double bogey". I smiled and didn't say another word because to me that was over and I had to move on and concentrate on the next tee shot.

I hit a great driver down the middle of the very narrow fairway on the par 5, 11th hole. I then hit my fairway wood to 10 feet and made the putt for eagle. As we walked off the green, I turned to my friend, smiled and simply said "That's how."

To be honest, I vaguely remembered this story but I ran into my friend about ten years after that incident and he retold me the story. He said that it forever changed the way he felt about handling adversity and he actually thanked me for the lesson.

One of the best things we can do in life is to learn from our mistakes. Since we are far from perfect, there are a lot of mistakes made in any given round of golf. The *trick* is to dust yourself off and get right back up on that horse, once its thrown you off. Learn from your mistakes and you'll make a lot less of them in the future but be aware there will be more mistakes to be made.

I'm going to let you in on a little secret, even the best players in the world make mistakes all the time. Sure it seems like when you're watching the final round on TV those guys never miss a shot and make every putt. I suppose that's why you're watching them on Sunday. The truth is they only show you the made putts and great shots on TV. The rest of the field is struggling just to improve their position, because winning or even getting any TV time is out of the question at a certain point. Go watch a professional golf tournament in person and you may see shots that you might think to yourself "I could have done better that!".

Golf is a marathon, not a sprint. If you make a mistake, usually you can recover. If your mistake happens on the last hole and it costs you the match or tournament, learn from it and next time you should have a better result.

There is no better example of this than what 21 year old Rory McIlroy did in the 2011 Masters and US Open.

I was fortunate enough to be at Augusta National that year to witness this amazing tournament. He was dominant in the Masters that year for 63 holes and then the wheels absolutely fell off. He triple bogeyed the 10th hole and you've never seen anyone unravel so completely. He finished with a round of 80 including going 7 over par the final nine holes. It was painful to watch such a fine young man collapse the way he did and at one point he even appeared to be in tears.

An amazing thing happened after the round. He sat down with the media and answered every painful question with dignity and class, showing his true character and a maturity beyond his years. He vowed to learn from his experience. It was an impressive display of poise to behold. I was very proud of the young man and I knew he would recover quickly from this meltdown. What happened next was that young Mr. McIlroy showed his skeptics a display of golf not seen since Tiger Woods 15 shot dominance in the 2000 US Open. McIlroy faced up to his mistakes, learned from them and won the 2011 US Open by 8 shots (and it really wasn't even that close).

So you see, things do go wrong but it's how we handle ourselves when things don't go as planned which determines our success in the future. Strive for perfection but allow yourself to be imperfect and the imperfections won't destroy you.

When mistakes happen, what's the best way to proceed? Here are six simple steps to follow:

1) *Accept it and move on.* You have no control over what just happened but you do have a say in what happens next.

2) *Breathe.* Take a few deep cleansing breaths and let the tension leave your body. This will assist you in slowing your heart rate.

3) *Regain your focus.* Stay calm and get back to the rhythm of your game. Walk slower and relax. Before you hit your next shot, make sure that you fully reset yourself and get back to your normal pre-shot routine.

4) *Erase the video.* Every golfer has to have short term memory loss to be great. Learn the ability to erase the previous shot from your mind and use your 5 Sense Imagery to help you refocus on the next shot. 5 Sense Imagery requires such intense focus that you'll have no room in your mind to think about what just happened and will center you only on the task at hand.

5) *Love the adversity.* Think of it as an opportunity for greatness. How many times have you hit an amazing recovery shot from an extremely difficult spot and had a rush of adrenaline because of it. It's a great feeling to pull off a difficult shot but difficult shots are usually preceded by a mistake we made

that put us in that difficult position in the first place. *Remember, an amazing shot might be a simple chip out into the fairway which is then followed by the great shot. Don't compound the original mistake by immediately making another one if the shot just isn't there.*

6) *Smile and have fun.* The thing I think most players forget (especially when the pressure level is extremely high) is that this game is supposed to be fun! Learn to laugh at yourself or at least don't take yourself so seriously, it is just a game after all. When a mistake happens, smile or even laugh and your troubles won't seem so daunting. Remember the word *perspective,* because in the grand scheme of things life could always be worse. Learn to have fun and enjoy yourself.

Follow these six simple steps to dealing with mistakes and you might begin to notice that fewer mistakes will follow. This is because you'll stop seeing the things you do on a golf course as *good* or *bad*, just something that needs to be accepted.

Chapter 4

GOLFING YOUR BALL:
The Art of the Process

Around the world, futbol or what we Americans know as soccer is called "The Beautiful Game". Sorry, but to me golf is the most beautiful of all games. Golf has been around for centuries and is now played by hundreds of millions of people from every corner of the planet.

The game is played on some of the most pristine pieces of land anywhere. One only has to step foot onto 17 Mile Drive in California's Monterey Peninsula to know what heaven must look like, or at least a golfer's heaven! Each golf course, each hole, each shot is distinctly different from the next. My 19 year old daughter is a wonderful artist and in her first year of college at the prestigious Art Center College of Design, in Pasadena. I try to guide her future with my best fatherly advice. I always use the similarities between the art world and the golf world to help her understand what awaits her in the future. As an ex-professional golfer, I understand the sacrifices one has to make to succeed at the highest level. The long hours in the hot sun, practicing until it hurts. Struggling from paycheck to paycheck and wondering if it's all worth the immense effort. I could easily see the comparison to a struggling artist. We, the golfer and the artist, work tirelessly perfecting our craft. We both are chronic dream chasers and love the journey as much as arriving at the destination. We struggle to make ends meet or reap the incredible rewards if we are truly successful. We are perfectionists and are seldom satisfied with our work. An artist uses the brush to paint something beautiful on canvas and a golfer uses clubs to create a work of art on the course. Undoubtedly though, the greatest similarity between the artist and the golfer is that to be successful you *must* love doing what you do.

Golf is, in its most basic form, a kind of performance art. The golfer uses imagination like an artist, seeing the vision of a beautiful shot before striking the ball. Fluid and powerful movements are used to create a dance-like action. The golfer's swing, when done correctly, is a form of poetry and grace. To me, the sight of a perfectly struck golf shot and DaVinci's "Mona Lisa" are equally impressive.

There is an art to playing the game of golf. There must be flow, rhythm, peacefulness, and strength to your movements and an incredible amount of imagination is required.

Throughout this chapter I will explain practical requirements needed to raise your game to it's highest level, how to actually play the game during a round as it relates to the Process, and why some personality traits are more conducive to success than others.

PRE-ROUND PREPARATION

I remember in my early playing days as a pro, I would get up, take a quick shower, throw on the first appropriate articles of clothing, grab a power bar and race out the door. Driving rapidly to the course, I would get out of the car, slap on my shoes and head for the driving range. I would hit the minimal number of range balls required to loosen up my back (if I had that much time) and head for the putting green to hit about two minutes of putts just to get a sense of the green's speed. Often I would play wonderfully but sometimes I would get off to a slow start and struggled to recover the rest of the day.

I learned early on that to be successful at the professional level one must be properly prepared for whatever might be encountered that day.

Proper preparation begins the day before your round. It might begin right after your previous days round has ended. This is why you'll see tour players head to the range after the round, even if they played well. They are trying to correct a certain swing flaw that may have popped up that day or just trying to keep the rhythm going for tomorrows round. I must admit, I did this very infrequently as I constantly had to protect my back from over use. I made up for this lack of post-round practice by hitting balls on off days but mostly I worked harder on my mental preparation than anyone else.

After most rounds I would find a quiet confortable place and do about 30 minutes of self-hypnosis and 15 to 30 minutes of breathing meditation to re-center myself. Added to this mental work was 3 to 5 days a week of physical training in the gym. The player with a sound mind and sound body has the best chance for success.

Next comes the all important down time. A nice hot shower and a quiet night with a good book in bed or an occasional night out for a drink or two with my mates was the common evening. It's good to mix up your down time as to not make your life too monotonous.

It's important not to over indulge, as you'll need to be clear headed and alert when you wake up the next morning.

Every night before a round of golf I would play the entire golf course in my head before I went to sleep. Some nights I would spend as much as two hours playing that round, while other nights I would fall asleep after a couple of holes. This would accomplish two goals, first it would be great mental training and second it would give me a good sense of strategy for the way I was going to play the course the next day.

Of course I never played the golf course in reality the way I did the night before in my mind but I did come close in some rounds. If I played the way I did in my mind, you wouldn't be reading this book, you would be watching me win every tournament on TV. For you see, in my mind I play perfectly. Every tee shot splits the fairway, every iron shot flies at the flag, and every putt goes in dead center of the hole. I have had quite a few rounds in which I split every fairway and even hit every green but the lowest round I ever shot was 10 under par. Again, it's not important that you replicate the imaginary round of perfection, only that you step on the tee of every hole with that intention.

Another important aspect of pre-round preparation is rest. Make sure you get enough sleep before an important round of golf. This game requires an enormous amount of energy, both mental and physical and enough rest is crucial to having a heightened sense of focus.

It's game day and you are ready to go because you began your preparation for this day, yesterday. You got enough sleep and you set your alarm clock early enough to get everything done without rushing around in the morning. Early rising isn't as important for afternoon rounds but for the early morning round proper preparation is a major key to a successful day on the links.

Here is my morning routine before a tournament.

1) Set the alarm clock to give me two hours prep time (not counting transit time). Yes this means that even if your tee time is 6:30am you will be up very early so it's very important that you get to sleep early the night before.

2) I take a hot shower to loosen up my back and eat a healthy but not too filling breakfast (It is the most important meal of the day they say).

3) I give myself plenty of transit time so I won't have to rush and throw off my natural rhythm...or get a speeding ticket.

4) Once I arrive at the course, I find a quiet place to do 15 minutes of breathing meditation to clear my mind.

5) After cleansing my mind, I do 5 to 15 minutes of stretching or warm up drills depending on the weather (cold weather requires more time to warm up). Stretching tends to aggravate my back at times so I prefer to get the blood flowing by running in place, doing jumping jacks or push-ups and sit-ups.

6) Now I have about 45 minutes to hit balls, work on the short game and putting, again without hurrying about. I never ever leave the putting green without making four 3 foot putts in a row. This is an important part of my routine because it builds the confidence to see the ball go in the hole that many times in a row.

Once I played a tournament in Asia and after about ten tries, I still hadn't made my four 3 footers in a row and usually it never takes more than three times to accomplish this feat. I heard them announce my name on the first tee. One of my friends told me I better get up there quick or I might be DQ'ed, but I was unflustered and didn't let that distract me. Finally I had made three in a row and I actually felt pressure to make the last putt. I lined it up, knocked it in and ran to the first tee. My friend knowing my routine was cracking up and I could hear him laughing all the way to the tee. The starter gave me a dirty look and told me to hit away immediately. I didn't miss one putt inside of 10 feet that day.

7) Except for that round in Asia I always made it to the first tee just as the prior group teed off. This allowed me time to retrieve from my golf bag a pre-marked golf ball, enough tees and a ball marker for the round. I would neatly fold the hole location sheet into thirds and place it in my yardage guide. I go

over the rules sheet and greet my playing partners with a smile and "Hello".

Thus ends my pre-round preparation. Now I've done everything I can to ensure confidence and remove any bad thoughts that inevitably come with poor preparation.
Now it's time to hit one shot at a time with the knowledge that by following my Process, success is a certainty.
Seven steps to pre-round preparation worked for me but everyone is different. You might find that 45 minutes isn't enough or is too much practice before a round. Maybe you need an hour to meditate, stretch, or hit balls. It's important that you develop your own routine and follow it every time.
Remember, repetition is fundamental to success in golf.

YOUR EQUIPMENT

Your golf equipment is the most subjective part of your game or this book. There is no way I can tell you what clubs to place in your bag, as only you know what works best for you. Any of the major golf companies can provide quality equipment to help elevate your game to peak performance levels.

What I can tell you is how to match your set for it's greatest effectiveness.

In my college golf days of the mid '80's, I used a set of blade irons 2-pw, a driver, a 3 wood, two sand wedges, and a putter. I was an exceptional long iron player and had great distance control with those irons. Wedges back then were different than today. They were gap, sand, or lob wedges and unless you really knew what you were doing you had no idea what their lofts were. Today, most players have three or even four wedges in their bag.

If you look back at an older persimmon (that's "wood" to you younger players) or even the first generation of steel headed drivers, they look so tiny you wonder how you could have ever hit them. It makes what great players like Bobby Jones, Ben Hogan, Arnold Palmer, and Jack Nicklaus did so impressive. I challenge any of the younger players to grab a wooden driver and go to the range to hit a few balls. You'll be amazed at just how good the players of the past were.

With the advancements in todays technology, present day golfers are spoiled with equipment that nearly hits itself. Drivers have 460cc heads that are the size of basketballs.

Hybrids now replace long irons as they fly higher and are easier to hit. Wedges come in every degree of loft and bounce. Irons are perimeter weighted which creates a larger sweet spot for straighter shots and improved distance with off center shots. Putters are made in every shape, material, length, and grip size. It's almost as if we have no more excuses for our bad play.

The absolute biggest change in equipment though, is the advancements in the golf ball itself. Today's golf ball flies significantly farther and straighter, and is much more durable than the golf ball of even 15 years ago.

You would think that all these changes to today's equipment would make the game so much easier but it has also produced a change in the way golf courses are now built and set up. Great courses of the past hundred years, like Merion or Cypress Point, are still great but they have been made nearly obsolete because they just aren't long enough to accommodate today's players and equipment. Some courses like Augusta National have been lengthened to keep up. Newer courses are designed longer more narrow and overall much more difficult, so we have to design our golf bag to fit each course we are about to play.

Before any tournament I would play practice rounds to decide what golf set configuration would work best for this particular course. Some courses are shorter and eliminate the need for long irons or hybrids so I would add an extra wedge. There was a time when Phil Mickelson would use two drivers on courses that had lots of doglegs, one for left to right tee shots and one for right to left tee shots.

The point is that you are allowed to use 14 clubs and you need to decide which clubs will be used the most, then set your bag up appropriately for each different golf course. In my bag at the moment is a 9 degree driver, 15.5 degree 3 wood, an 18 degree hybrid, 4-pw forged cavity back irons, a 52, 56, and 60 degree wedge set, and a center shafted 38" putter (I use a longer putter so I don't have to bend over as much when I putt to save my back). This is my standard set but I have no problem adding or subtracting any club to my set to help better fit the course I'm about to play.

I must now talk about some of the pitfalls of equipment. On tour, most all players have lucrative club contracts. This doesn't stop the golf club company reps from attempting to give you free clubs to try in hopes that you'll put it in your bag so that they can get it in the tournament count. Club counts in tournaments are crucial to the golf companies future sales. They pay players just to use their equipment. In fact on the first tee of every tournament there is an independent company there to count and label every club in your bag. They do this to let the companies know who is actually using their equipment, to let the companies know who to pay and how much, and to get the numbers so they can post them in their advertisements.

As an ex-touring professional I have a garage full of golf clubs I've been given from the reps throughout the years. There is even a saying used by some of the tour players, "If it's free I'll take three, if there's more I'll take four!". A friend of mine was looking through my garage and he called me "Noah" because I had two of everything!

Free stuff sounds great but there is a catch. Before I qualified for the Nationwide Tour in the late ninety's (then it was called the Nike Tour), an experienced player warned me about the *addiction* of free equipment. He gave me some great advise, "Dance with the girl you brought to the prom". What this means is that the temptation to use all the free stuff they give you is powerful, but the clubs in my bag are the ones that got me to the tour and I should stick with them. Sadly I gave into the temptation and changed everything. It took some time to adjust to the new equipment and that cost me valuable weeks out there until I felt comfortable with all of my new goodies.

The great thing about getting on that tour and making some of the changes I did was learning about club fitting. Club fitting is an essential factor in getting the absolute most out of your game. You could have the best golf swing in the world but if your equipment doesn't fit, it could cost you a lot of strokes. The most obvious example would be if your swing speed is 110 mph and you were using a regular flex shaft. That swing speed is way too much for a regular shaft and you will most likely hit the ball with too much spin which causes high off line shots. Conversely, if you use an extra stiff shaft and your swing speed is 80 mph, you won't generate enough speed to flex the shaft properly and you will hit the ball with less spin and a much shorter distance. Other important things to know about proper club fitting is the length of clubs, the lie, and loft. I'm 6'4" and have always use +1/2" length clubs. This allows me to keep the correct posture throughout the swing. I have my clubs made 1 degree upright because I'm taller.

A way to see if you have the correct lie is to check your divots. If your clubs are too upright, you'll see heel heavy divots and if they are too flat you'll see toe heavy divots. A perfect divot should be shallow, evenly distributed and look about the size of a dollar bill.

Lofts are determined by your swing and ball flight. I have always had a lower ball flight, so I use standard lofts in my driver, 3 wood, and irons. Some players with extreme ball flights will need to make adjustments in loft to level out their flight. Proper spin ratios will add maximum distance to your game. The best thing to do is go get fitted from a professional club fitter, as this can make all the difference in your game.

In today's game, golf equipment is like computer equipment in that the advancements in innovation happen so rapidly that last years models are rendered nearly obsolete by the new products. Players have to keep up with the latest technologies, so you have to make changes to your bag almost every year. That's why, with the exception of your putter, I would recommend not falling in love with any piece of equipment in your bag. The gray area with all these changes is that you have to decide if a few extra yards is really worth some of the uncertainties created with constant change.

I recently upgraded my driver. My friends thought I was crazy because I hit the one I had so straight, but they were all hitting their drivers as far or farther than mine. Of course this had to be the fault of the driver, it *couldn't* be me. Well after a few shaky rounds with the new driver, I now hit it just as straight but almost 15 yards farther. The new improvements from technology are really amazing. So like I said to begin this section about equipment, it's really a subjective topic. Whatever you feel works best for you is ultimately the best decision. Just be sure that your equipment is fitted especially for your game.

SKILL SHOTS

In any given round of golf, you're most likely hitting what I call *driving range* shots. What this means is if your standard 7 iron shot flies 160 yards and you are in the middle of the fairway with that distance to the hole, you're going to hit a *driving range* 7 iron. Most shots we hit in a round are standard shots but often the difference in a good or great round is how you handle the *skill shots.*

I define a *skill shot* as any shot which requires a different swing than your normal motion. If you normal ball flight is a 5 yard fade and you now have to hit a 10 yard draw, to you that would be a skill shot.

The problem with the average golfer is that they rarely if ever practice skill shots. You can go to any driving range and all you'll see is people working on their swings, hitting the same shot over and over again. Not that this is a terrible thing, as a good repetitive swing is essential. But you must practice the skill shots so that you'll know what to do during a round when these unusual situations inevitably arise.

When I play with my friends who are all single digit or scratch handicap amateur golfers, I see the same mistakes all the time. They are often rolling through a round and playing very well and then it happens, they are confronted with a shot they rarely practice.

This is when they try to get creative and invent a shot they have no idea how to pull off. If you want to see a round go south in a hurry, try to hit a shot you've never hit before. The usual outcome is a poorly struck and misdirected golf shot. These are the shots that head for the OB stakes or water or into the tree in front of them and straight down or worse. What should be a chance for par or bogey at worst, turns into double and triple bogeys, which is a really quick way to kill momentum and ruin a good round.

I recommend setting aside at least 30 balls from your practice session to use your imagination. Practice hitting low and high hooks, low and high fades, high straight shots and low straight shots. Try hitting a 7 iron 50 yards, 80 yards, and 120 yards as these are the shots you'll need when hitting out of the trees.

It's extremely important to practice unusual lies. Don't always hit every practice session shot from a perfect flat lie. Place balls in divots and sandy lies and see how the ball reacts out of those lies. Hit shots out of the long grass and on uneven lies such as when the ball is below your feet and above your feet or uphill and downhill lies. Take a bucket of balls to the practice sand area and hit shots from 30 to 200 yards.

Knowing how the ball reacts from all these different lies can fill your memory bank and help to create a confident feeling when confronted with that situation during a critical moment of any given round.

I can remember many times being on a driving range, just devoting an entire practice session to hitting unusual type skill shots. I would turn around from time to time, just to see all the strange looks on the people's faces who were watching me. Often they would offer advice to help me hit a shot straight not knowing that I was doing exactly what I was trying to do. Apparently it's very strange to do anything on a driving range other than to hit the same shot over and over again.

Don't be afraid to try new things or even to look less than perfect while practicing. Have fun with it and I promise that you will have the last laugh. It will feel especially rewarding when all that practice pays off at a critical moment in a round, when you hit an amazing recovery shot. You will feel proud of yourself for taking the time to learn how to hit the skill shots and when you pull these shots off, you'll find a continuance in momentum and a rise in confidence.

There are so many combinations of golf shots that you could hit in a given round or tournament. The more prepared you are for the skill shot the better the results.

HANDLING THE CONDITIONS

In my golfing career, I won more than 40 tournaments. I would say that probably half of those were won under adverse weather conditions. I absolutely love playing golf in the worst conditions imaginable. My love for difficult playing conditions goes back to my teenage years when my father told me something I've never forgotten. He said "If you can learn to love playing in conditions that most others hate, you've already beaten them". Even as a kid that made a lot sense. I didn't *fully* understand what he meant until my college senior year conference championships.

It was a three day tournament at Lake Shastina Golf Course at the foot of Mt. Shasta in Northern California. I remember on the night before the tournament, I was looking out the window of my hotel room and watching the three freshmen on my team playing in the snow in the parking lot. Being from Southern California their whole life, they had never seen falling snow and wanted to have fun. Crazy freshmen!

The next morning there was a frost delay before the tournament and every single player was in the beautiful clubhouse, sitting in front of the fire complaining about how cold it was. I stood alone at the doorway listening to all the complaining and thought to myself, "I've already won this tournament". I went outside all by myself to warm up in the freezing damp weather and hit balls with a big smile on my face. I led wire to wire and not only did I win the tournament but my team won as well earning us a trip to Tampa, Florida for the NCAA Div.II Championships (won by Lee Jansen).

I saw the look in those collegiate players eyes and knew I had the advantage. I've played in hundreds of pro tournaments and saw that same look every time the weather conditions got particularly nasty. It was almost as if I would feed on their fear and gain strength from their weakness.

I used to go into the locker room on cloudy days and jokingly do rain dances just to tease my fellow competitors. I never want to see anyone in pain and I wouldn't recommend gaining happiness from others misery but I would say that if someone willingly gives up their energy, don't feel bad taking it from them.

RAIN

Now lets talk about how specifically to deal with certain weather conditions. Rain is the most difficult of all conditions to play in because not only does it affect ball flight but it affects your handle on the club. Rain requires an amazing amount of preparation and patience. Depending on the amount of rain and its duration, you'll need an extra towel or two, at least five clean gloves in a plastic zip lock bag, a good umbrella, properly fitted waterproof rain pants and jacket, a club cover for your golf bag to keep your clubs dry, and good all weather shoes. Next you'll need patience, lots and lots of patience. Never should you hit a shot in golf without completely being prepared, but in the rain that fact is magnified ten fold.

If your not ready to play any shot in the rain, you're asking for trouble. All the club has to do is slip an eighth of an inch and the ball could go anywhere. Before you hit any shot in the rain, make sure your grips and your glove are as dry as you can make them and that you feel as connected to the club as possible.

The key to successful play in the rain is to take an extra club and hit every shot at no more than three quarters speed. Never try to hit full shots in the rain. You will have less slippage and more solid contact. Solid contact is without a doubt the most important thing when playing in adverse weather conditions whether it be wind, rain, heat or cold. Just another reason to work on skill shots, such as three quarter swings in your practice sessions. I would even put on a glove and dunk it in a bucket of water, then hit shots on the range just to get a sense of hitting shots with a wet glove.

Everything takes longer to do in the rain. You have to keep things as dry as possible and that takes time. You have to deal with your umbrella and your gear and you have to deal with the other players who will themselves be playing slower. Be prepared for a long day in the rain and if you are, you'll be able to focus on what matters most, the shot before you.

WIND
Everyone seems to have their own way of dealing with wind but there are a few things you need to know. The most important thing to know about playing golf in the wind is that everyone else has to deal with it equally. The wind plays no favorites and everyone else is likely struggling as well, so remember to have patience and try to enjoy the challenge.

My theory for playing in the wind is not to do anything too different with my swing. I don't try to hit it higher or lower or shape my shots just to ride the wind or hold shots against the wind. I just hit my normal shot and take into account how much I will have to allow for that amount of wind.

For example, if I had a 180 yard shot to the green and there was a 20 mph left to right cross wind, I would just hit a straight shot aiming 20 yards left of my target and let the wind blow the ball back to the hole.

Same thing if you're hitting directly into the wind. If there is a 20 mph wind in your face, don't try to hit the ball lower just hit your normal shot and add about 20 yards to your distance.

If you try to hit the ball lower, usually you will trap shots and that adds spin to the ball which will cause your ball to float or rise and be more at the mercy of the wind. Floating or rising balls come up well short. When hitting shots downwind, the wind will take spin off and the ball again will fall short. Most people think that hitting a ball downwind will automatically cause the ball to fly much farther which isn't always true. Yes the ball does fly farther downwind but it depends on how much spin you can put on the ball. Rotation of the golf ball is what keeps it in the air. Shots out of the rough or longer iron or wood shots won't always fly as far in comparison to a well struck iron shot from the fairway.

The aerodynamics of golf ball flight is immensely complex and probably a bit above my grade scale but it is something that you're going to want to learn a little about to prevent you from airmailing a green by 30 yards.

Unless necessary, I don't try to shape shots in the wind, as poorly hit shots are exaggeratedly pushed off line and harder to control. It's tough enough to control the ball flight of a shaped shot in the wind even when shots are solidly struck.

A great golfer once told me that he doesn't do anything different in the wind except add or subtract distance or change aiming points. He said "Why would I try to hit shots that I almost never practice just because it's windy!". I agreed but asked him why doesn't he practice hitting wind shots on the range? He said he does but he felt that he had more confidence using the swing he practices the majority of the time. I would say that whatever brings you the most confidence is what you should use in that moment.

HEAT

Playing years in Asia and in the southern United States in the summer taught me the importance of hydration. I've never been so hot as I was at the Asian PGA Qualifying School in Melacca, Malaysia. It was 105 degrees fahrenheit and 100% humidity. The heat there was oppressive and I got a minor case of heat stroke in the practice round. The doctor's had to put me on an I.V. drip to keep my body hydrated.

When playing in the heat, make sure you drink plenty of water. The general rule is that no matter how much you drink, if you're not urinating, you're not drinking enough. For the next four days of that Q-School in Malaysia, I amazingly drank one bottled water for every hole I played.

Wearing the right sun block and keeping the sun off your skin and head are also important, so get a good hat and keep sun block in a plastic zip-lock bag in your golf bag.

Another important thing to note about playing in the heat or at higher altitudes is that the ball will travel farther distances. The air is thinner and produces less resistance. Practice rounds will help to determine how much farther the ball will travel. I played a tournament in Toluca, Mexico which is about 7,000 above sea level. I calculated that I needed to add about 12% extra yardage. So for example, if I had 224 yards to the hole, I would hit my 200 yard club.

COLD
The cold for me is even tougher than playing in the heat. I have long thin fingers that are susceptible to the cold. I hate the feel of a missed hit shot in the cold because it hurts so bad. It's a really good incentive to focus on solid ball contact.
The remedy is to get the best cold weather gear available and wear protective cold weather gloves between shots to keep your hands as warm as possible.
With cold weather, the air is much more dense and it's harder to compress the golf ball, which produces shorter shots. At about 40*F, the ball will travel about 8-10% less the actual yardage.
To sum up, playing golf in adverse weather conditions is all about preparation, patience, and knowledge but there is one other thing, toughness! Most anyone can play well and have a good time

when condition are ideal but it takes a certain mental toughness to play in difficult conditions. With a strong Process in place and a learned ability to bare down, stay positive, be patient, and focus intensely in the moment, you will find an inner toughness that grows stronger every day. The more you work on your Process the stronger you'll become, and you'll gain an edge in adverse conditions.

COURSE MANAGEMENT

Once upon a time there used to be a concept known as *Course Management.* 30 years ago, the golf commentators used to talk about it all the time. I remember my college golf coach blabbing on and on about it. I would map out intricate strategies before every round I played as an amateur and I would try to stick to that plan on every hole.
A funny thing happened in the past fifteen years, course management went the way of the beeper. It seems now that the modern day golfer hits the ball so far that they pull out a driver on every hole and swing as hard as they can. Their strategy seems to be, better to hit a driver off the tee and leave only a pitching wedge from the rough than to hit 3 wood off the tee and be left with a 7 iron from the fairway.

Players such as John Daly and Tiger Woods glamorized the long ball. Suddenly everyone wanted to hit drivers 300+ yards and throw caution to the wind.

I'll break it down even further. I attribute Tiger Woods for the changes in the modern game of golf. He's the reason the golfer of today is so damn good. When I grew up in the late 70's and early 80's, golf was a game for the kids that just weren't athletic enough to play football or basketball. The high school golf team member of my day looked more like a member of the schools Science Club. No self respecting athletic teen would be caught dead playing golf unless his father dragged him out to the country club like the character *Spaulding* in the movie "Caddyshack".

Every generation or so, there comes along a phenom who forever changes the game. Babe Ruth, Jim Brown, Wayne Gretzky, Michael Jordan all brought their respective sports to an unprecedented higher level. Then along came a skinny kid named Eldrick "Tiger" Woods to the golf world.

He was first seen on "The Johnny Carson Show" at age 2, dazzling Johnny and the studio audience with his golf swing. But it wasn't until 14 years later that he burst on the golf scene winning three US Amateur Championships in a row. Next he turned pro and won six tournaments his first 12 months on the PGA Tour.

He became such a shining star that every company in the world sought after him to endorse their products. He won the Masters by 12 strokes and the US Open by an unprecedented 15 strokes. No one could stop him and I don't think anyone will ever match the twelve year run he had.

It also didn't hurt his popularity that he was a young man of color. His ethnicity made everyone take a new look at the sport that had always catered to the affluent and usually white golfer.

Suddenly it was cool for anyone to play golf. The teen that would have been a star on his high school football or baseball team now thought "If Tiger Woods can make hundreds of millions of dollars playing golf, why should I risk killing myself playing football?".

They looked at Tiger as a super fit athletic mega star who's popularity and world recognition was only second to Mickey Mouse. It was amazing how quickly the game had changed.

Now if you look at the players on the PGA Tour, you'll see athletes, not fat guys in ugly pants (though they do still wear some pretty ugly pants!). The modern golfer is health conscious, physically agile and strong, well versed on the advantages of physical and mental training, nutrition, and the science of swing mechanics.

It seems like every tournament I play in now is filled with young players who hit the ball 50 yards by me, into places I don't dream of. I'm still nearly as competitive as the long driving kids because my Process is stronger, I have a maturity edge, and I still use an updated form of course management. All the talent in the world won't help you if you don't have a plan and stick to it. If you're looking for a good example of this is, watch a major championship.

The young world beaters come out hot and fast but in the end it usually seems like the seasoned grizzled veteran hangs on just long enough to win. Sure golf is changing rapidly and young golfers like Rory McIlroy should break this trend but it usually takes years of putting yourself in position to win before something clicks and you finally have that breakthrough moment.

Why does it take time to learn how to win the biggest tournaments? I believe it takes a long time to find the correct Process that works best for each individual golfer.

Most guys are out there continuously searching for what works best. They change their routines daily trying to find the magic secret that will finally put them over the top. This was the main reason I decided to write this book, to give players a Process to follow every day and to achieve stability in their golf and their lives.

Let's face it, with today's equipment, course management isn't quite as important as it used to be. Most golf courses can just simply be overpowered, but championship golf courses provide a whole different challenge. The proper Process, the right strategy, and an incredible mental toughness are what is required to conquer the most difficult challenges in the game of golf.

I remember the first time I played golf in Scotland. It was at a great golf course outside of Edinburgh called Gullane No.1 for the final stage of British Open qualifying in 2002.

I remember thinking about halfway through my practice round, "I'm playing *real* golf for the first time in my life!" This course required a definite, well thought out strategy. Every shot had to be placed in just the correct location or the consequences were very penal. You couldn't just grip it and rip it.

The second hole, for example, was a beautiful par 4 dogleg left and straight up a hill. This course's fairways were cut out of waist high grass, so my strategy was to hit 4 iron off the tee and hit 3 iron up the hill to the green. You could hit driver over the high grass to shorten the hole and hope to hit the fairway, which my two playing partners attempted, but this was a risky venture. I made par both days on the hole with my strategy, they both made double bogey both times with theirs.

America's newer golf courses are designed mostly for target golf. You hit to a spot in the fairway and then hit to a target in the correct quadrant of the green. In British links golf you have to manage your ball throughout invisible hazards, pothole bunkers, and uneven slopes. Most holes allow you to run your shot through an opening in the front of the green.

Rarely do you hit a flop shot or spin a ball back 15 feet like we do in the States. It's really two different games and requires two different course strategies. I felt my game was better suited for links golf because of my creativity, patience, and ability to handle tough weather conditions. Most links courses don't put such an importance on length off the tee, accuracy is the key.

CONSISTENCY AND STABILITY

If I got a dollar for every time someone called my golf game *boring* I would be a rich man. Countless times after a round I would be asked by my playing partners "What did you shot today?". When I would say 66, 67 or whatever my score would be, they would always say the same thing "You shot what? No way!". What they were really saying was that my game was so dull that nothing really stood out enough to warrant such a low score.

The player who hits booming long drives or makes unbelievable recovery shots from unusual places or fist pumps a good shot or screams profanities at his ball, they are the ones that leave a lasting impression. Players like me are easily forgettable and often fly under the radar, until it's time to collect the money or trophy.

Average length drives but in the fairway, iron shots on the green but not always bouncing off the flag stick, or only an occasional lengthy holed putt but only rarely a three putt or short misses, these are the attributes of the consistent and stable golfer.

I guess the best analogy would be "The Tortoise and the Hare". Slow and steadily just plodding along. Unassuming and content to let others rise and fall on their own emotional roller coasters.

If you think about it, what is the most important thing in the game of golf, it's repetition. To be repetitive is by definition to do the same thing over and over again. My favorite example of this type of player is Reteif Gossen in his prime. Beautiful fluid swing, long straight drives, great iron play, and amazing touch around the greens. He is a two-time US Open champion and yet he is considered the most boring of all players.

He could make a hole-in-one or quadruple bogey and you would never know the difference by his facial expressions or body language. What just happened is over with (good or bad) and now let's move on to the next situation. Methodically and calmly going about your business with no flash, ego, or theatrics, to me that is the most exciting of all players and here's why.

Anyone can get excited and pump fists or scream at the top of their lungs but it takes the internal fortitude of a consistent and stable player to keep their temperament at an even keel. It doesn't always make for exciting TV but who really cares.

I call this "The Beauty of Vanilla". I used to say "The Beauty of Boring" but I was told the word *boring* had more negative connotation than the word *vanilla*.

Players like Reteif, Luke Donald, Steve Stricker, or Dustin Johnson are great but slightly different examples of the "Vanilla" golfer. They are brilliant and fun to watch golfers who express few emotional highs or lows as they go about their business. Rarely do you see any inordinate amounts of emotions. They always seem to have a sense of control and calmness about them, and I mean all the time not just in one given round. They are aware that golf is a marathon and to get so emotional all the time would eventually burn them out.

Vanilla is not the most exciting flavor but it is versatile, easy to digest, and reliable. There are no surprises with a vanilla golf game, only a steady level headed and unflappable competitor.

Nothing ruffles their feathers because they rarely let the situation get the better of them. Excitable players are led about by their emotions, often riding an exhausting roller coaster of their own doing. Maybe in today's society where everyone seems to have a desire for their 15 minutes of fame, some may feel that the only way to stand out from the crowd is to be outrageous. One only has to watch any reality TV show to see just how foolish and desperate for attention these people can be. Wearing your emotions on your sleeve or acting the fool might get you noticed but it won't help you stay focused or help keep you firmly on your path. A well developed Process is the best way to the vanilla golf game. The Process will guide you in times of stress, fatigue, and will assist you in fighting off the negative emotions that constantly embattle or destroy the excitable golfer.

I did at times, but not often enough, shot rounds in the low 60's (though it was always my intention to go low) but it was even more rare for me to shoot rounds in the mid to upper 70's. My scores day in and day out were usually similar depending on the course. Easier courses were usually in the mid to high 60's and tougher courses were in the high 60's to low 70's. This wasn't my intended plan, it just seemed to work out that way.

If you follow the Process exactly the way it's supposed to be followed, you'll find yourself being a much more consistent golfer. Just by developing a proper routine you'll be setting yourself up to be more repetitive and consistent.

Learning acceptance will keep you on an even keel and allow you to go about your business to the best of your ability. If your focus is pin point, emotions such as anger or fear or even excitement will prove to be unnecessary and a stoic stability will become your only natural temperament.

Now I would like to address some common misconceptions I hear from players about their temperaments.

"I play much better when I get angry", Ridiculous! No one plays better for any sustained period of time if they can't eliminate or at least control their temper. They might bare down and focus a bit more on the next shot but that never lasts, because *that* focus always disappears and eventually turns back into anger. The Process doesn't work when we are angry or lose our cool.

"I play better when I fist pump and get excited about my play" To that I would say, "Act like you've been there before" or "Wasn't that your intention?". Why get excited about something that was your original intention.

I would say that this game is the most difficult of all sports and the accomplishment of something exceptional deserves a pat on the back or a bow to the crowd. But I only recommend that if you have the temperament to enjoy the moment for a minute and then be able to forget it and move on to the next situation.

Years ago while playing with a lifelong friend who is a very good amateur golfer, something happened that drives this point home. On the downhill 175 yard par 3, 13th hole at Industry Hills (Babe) GC in California, my friend hit a beautiful shot that took one bounce and rolled gently into the hole for his first hole-in-one. You've never seen anyone get so excited. The next hole is another par 3 up a hill and over a hazard. I tried to calm him down and told him to put that ball into his bag so he could put it in his trophy case at home. He was so excited that he told me, "Don't worry, I got it under control". He didn't. He teed that ball up on the next hole and proceeded to cold top it into the hazard never to be found again! His excitement quickly turned to depression. He told me many years later, he wished he would have listened to me but he let the moment get the better of him.

Most players don't have that ability and they allow themselves to experience great highs and great lows. Roller coasters can be fun and exciting in small doses but to live your life on one can be stressful and leave you feeling nauseous. In the long run it's the tortoise who wins the race.

Still I'm questioned by my younger students about robbing them of their true personalities. One student specifically asked (as a joke I hope) "What if my outgoing personality and quirky character don't lend to a quiet calm demeanor on the course? Should I still be as *boring* as you?"

He is a funny kid and he does have a point. Not everyone has the same personality and demeanor. Some are extraverts, introverts, passionate, or stoic, so to say there is one right way to behave might be a misconception. What I would say is, be as consistent as possible with whatever you feel is your true personality but work daily to achieve a centered calm state of mind. Eventually you'll discover that your game will become more vanilla, as emotions become less useful or important to the success of your game.

Work to be humble and gracious in victory and defeat. Treat your fellow competitors as you would want them to treat yourself. Have fun and love what you do or find something else you do love. Life is fleeting and just too short to waste a second doing something you don't absolutely love!

EXPECTATIONS VS. INTENTIONS

Earlier in "Pre-Round Preparation", I discussed the importance of playing rounds in your mind the night before a round. Again, it's not important that you replicate the imaginary round of perfection, only that you step on the tee of every hole with that intention.

It's important to distinguish the difference between "Intentions" and "Expectations". Intentions are the goals you put out to the universe without any attachments to the results. Expectations are the attachments to the results that we want to happen. For example, I have a 10 foot putt with 2 feet of break and the putt is straight downhill. My intention is to read the putt correctly, then start the ball on the right line and with the right speed. The result of this can only be that the ball goes in the hole but if doesn't, I'm willing to accept whatever the result might be. Only then can I freely move on to the next situation with a new intent for success.

If I have expectations my thought process would be to make the putt. I would only be concerned with the result. Sure I want to start the ball on the right line with the right speed but I'm more concerned with it going in or what would happen of it didn't. That attachment to the result leads to a few things.

First, if we are concerned about results we aren't in the moment. We are focused on a future event (the ball going in the hole) and we have no control over the future. Second, it can lead to disappointment when things don't go the way we *expect* them to and in turn this will ultimately lead to negativity and self pity.

Third, expectations lead us to *trying* instead of *doing*. There is an old Zen saying "Don't try, just do". Trying causes tension and places our focus again on the future. Doing leads to a freedom of thought directed only by in-the-moment thinking. A great example of this would be "The *B* Player". Ever seen a guy nervously set up to hit a tee shot on a narrow hole with out of bounds on both sides? You can almost predict the outcome. He *tries* to steer the ball down the fairway which forces a tight swing and a ball hit OB. Then he'll grab a provisional ball without thinking and rip it right down the middle. That's the *B* player doing it without expectations or pressure. The *B* player is a doer not a trier with a freeing detachment to the results. The trick is to put that freedom of detachment to the results into the mind of the *A* player.

Follow the Process and you'll learn the freedom of detachment from future results. You'll learn to let your intentions go out to the universe and be willing to live with whatever happens.

SELECTIVE MEMORY

I once had a wonderful debate with a friend about if we can learn from the past. It was his position that we couldn't because what happened in the past couldn't truly be replicated. Every situation in the present was new and required only what could be experienced in the here and now.

Of course I brought up obvious historical events like the holocaust or the great depression. "Don't you think we could learn from our past mistakes to insure that we don't duplicate them?" I reminded him of the saying "If we forget our past, we are doomed to relive it."

His contention was that if we continuously remember our past we can't escape it. His saying would be "Better to let bygones be bygones."

When it comes to golf, I think depending on the situation, both philosophies are true. There can be very little to be learned from having a ball hit a cart path and bounce out of bounds. In that situation there could be nothing better than to have *short term memory loss.*

Forget about unfortunate situations, just erase them from your mind forever and move on. There are just too many things that can happen in a round of golf that can cause grief if they aren't erased from memory. I can't think of a better attribute to keep your sanity in this game than to have short term memory loss.

There are also many situations where a good memory is absolutely essential to the improvement of your game. For example, one of the putting routines I have all my students incorporate into their game is to walk off distances from the hole.

Your mind is a powerful computer capable of storing billions of bits of information. Every time you walk off the distance of a putt, you store that in your memory bank so that the next time you have a similar putt you can recall that feeling. That is a perfect example of the necessity of a great memory. Another great example is how we handle past stressful situations, such as winning a big tournament or even losing one. It's comforting to recall a positive moment of when we won in a similar situation to the one you're currently in. Or to learn from how we handled ourself in a tough loss, so as to avoid making the same mistakes.

After years of thought about that debate with my friend concerning what we can or can't learn from the past, I've decided that the best approach would be to have "Selective Memory". Filter out all of the negative thoughts and let the positive thoughts be etched into your memory.

My father has *selective hearing.* He only hears what he wants to hear and it used to infuriate me! Now I see that this is his twisted way of having selective memory.

He doesn't even let the thought enter his head if he doesn't want to hear about it. What a gift it would be to be able to filter out the negativity of the world and only see or hear the positive.

A golfer with that kind of focus is a formidable opponent. Could you imagine if everything you saw or heard was positive and everything negative was simply ignored.

Well I'll tell you that not only is that possible but it's essential to success in your golf game.

The daily grind of a golfer's life can lead to fatigue or even burn out if you let it. I can't tell you how many great golfers I've know throughout the years that just let this game make them insane. They looked run down and fatigued all the time. They really did love the game but they just couldn't seem to find a way to not let it get to them.

It's a marathon not a sprint but in every marathon there is a point where some runners hit "the wall". This is a point about three quarters through the race when a decision must be made. "Do I quit or persevere?" I've seen so many get to that point and quit.

Burn out is a real problem amongst golfers. Golf is so darn difficult that if you allow it, the game will get the better of you. There is a saying "If you want to see a man's true character, play a round of golf with him!".

It's so true that this game can bring out your inner demons and show who you really are. I've seen golfers from all walks of life throw expensive clubs into lakes, scream profanities at the top of their lungs or rant and rave like a 2 year old who didn't get their way.

That's why it's imperative that you develop a strong Process. The Process enables you to deal with the daily grind because if your following it correctly, you will never feel the grind at all.

Speaking of grinding, let me tell about a particular golfer know as the "Grinder". These are the guys who look as if they have twenty thoughts flowing through their head at once. The grinder has a deliberate game (which is a polite way of saying they are unmercifully slow!).

They stand over a two foot putt forever as to ensure that they won't miss it. It's all we can do to keep from yelling at them "It's a two foot putt, what's there to think about!" The Grinder is overly cerebral and can't do anything without analyzing it to death.

Now there are certain moments that require a bit more attention but not every single shot of every single round. The longevity of the grinders life in the game is short and inevitably they burn out unless they find a way to change.

I won't lie, every golfer faces their own trials and tribulations with this game but it's the golfers with the strongest Process that perseveres even when confronted with *the wall.* Keep your thoughts and your Process simple. Use selective memory to stay positive and this will help you to stay fresh and create an effortless flow to your life and your game.

FROM GREAT HEIGHTS COME GREAT FALLS

Sports in general, evoke powerful emotions. Amazing drama, nail biting anxiety, and chilling thrills. Kurt Gibson's home run in the 1988 World Series, the U.S. Hockey team's "Miracle on Ice" victory over the powerhouse Russian team in the 1980 Winter Olympics, and Jack Nicklaus' unbelievable win at age 46 in the 1986 Masters are forever etched in our memory.

It would be next to impossible to remain level headed and stoic if you were involved in one of these great sports moments. Heck, it would be hard to watch on TV and not be out of your mind with excitement. Those three sporting moments were probably the most memorable to me.

Until the day I die, I'll never forget the day Gibson hit that home run. Being a lifelong Dodger fan I just had to go out to a local sports bar to watch game 1 of that 1988 World Series.

The place was packed with about 350 rabid Dodger fans and maybe 40 Oakland A's fans. The A's fans were loud the whole way as the A's were a dominant team and led the entire game. In the bottom of the ninth when all looked lost, the camera showed Gibson with a bat in his hands in the back of the dugout and the place erupted.

When he came to the plate on two bad legs, even Hollywood couldn't have written such an unbelievable story of what was about to happen. When he hit the ball over the right field fence, beer flew in the air and a deafening roar went through the sports bar. It brings chills to the back of my neck just to think about today.

This is the power of athletic competition. Sadly though there is a dark side to some sporting competitions. Bill Buckner's error in the 1986 World Series changed his life forever. Buckner was at the end of a very solid, long career in baseball. In game 6 the Boston Red Sox had the series in their grasp for the first time since 1918, when a routine ground ball was hit towards Buckner at first base. He probably shouldn't have been in the game in the ninth inning as he wasn't a great fielder. Sadly, this was proven when a routine ground ball rolled through his legs and the Red Sox lost the game. They went on to lose game 7 and the "Curse of the Bambino" lived on.

Buckner was one of the most liked players in the game but this didn't stop some idiot fans from sending him hundreds of death threats. He basically went into hiding all because of one mistake at an inopportune moment of a long productive career.

I could go on to list a dozen other so called *tragedies* in athletics but nothing represents *real* tragedy more than the story of Andres Escobar of the 1994 Colombian World Cup futbol team.

From a country in turmoil, Escobar was not only the star of the team, he was one of the most beloved citizens of Colombia. In that World Cup the Colombian team was the favorite. They were stunningly upset in the first game and played the host team USA in their second match. Needing a win to move on and avoid humiliation, an amazing thing happened.

The underdog team from the USA passed a ball in front of the Colombia's net and Andres Escobar accidentally kicked the ball in his own goal. Shocked, the team never recovered and lost another stunning upset and was eliminate from the tournament.

Here is when sport crosses the line and becomes something more than just another game. Escobar went home to Colombia and showing what amazing character he had, went out to face the public and take the inevitable criticism. Against the warnings of his teammates and family, he went out that night never to return. He was gunned down by a mob of cowardly so called *fans.* Some insist it was an organized hit. Either way, this was a tragedy in the truest sense of the word.

Why do I tell these stories of the highest highs and the lowest lows? I want to illustrate the importance of what really matters in life. Games, athletics, and sports are supposed to be fun. They are to be enjoyed or to be used to better yourself and the people around you.

Please don't take things so seriously. Learn perspective and try to keep a level head. When you live your life with your priorities in check, you will float gently down stream instead of constantly fighting against the current of your emotions.

Sure we would all dream of being Kurt Gibson or Jack Nicklaus at the moment of glory but to be the hero you must be willing to be the goat. It takes a hero, or a masochist, to truly handle the great highs and great lows.

This is why in golf or in life you must establish a powerful Process to get you through the tough times and even through the good times. I believe it can be as challenging to deal with good times as it is to handle the tough times. We all have had times of painful loss or failure. Usually we pick ourselves up, dust off and persevere.

Few of us are fortunate enough to experience championship moments or windfall gains. I could tell of countless examples of lottery winners who had their lives ruined by their amazing prosperity or athletes who just weren't ready and were crushed by the bright lights of fame and fortune. These are stories of people without the foundation of a strong Process.

I went into detail about being consistent, stable, and having a vanilla game and the stories I've just illustrated are perfect examples of why.

If you develop a strong Process, have the talent, and you're willing to put in the work, you better be prepared, because the bright lights of fame will find you. Here's the good news though, the Process will be your guide for a solid path to success. You will be able to handle the perceived good and bad times, and you'll be able to enjoy the journey it will most certainly take you on.

WHEN TO *THROW CAUTION TO THE WIND*

By this point in the book you've learned the importance of consistency and stability, mostly because I've said it a dozen times. I pride myself as an under the radar type player with a strong Process and even temperament. I rarely get excited or upset. I plod along like the tortoise and often just get to the finish line before the young hare. I enjoy the ease of my game and seldom if ever get burned out.

I learned to have a flow to my stride and my game. People often tell me that my golf game looks so effortless. You will commonly hear me joke "This game is so easy!" but that's because I know something a lot of golfers don't know, golf is easy, even when it's not.

I have (after a lot of painful lessons) learned the importance of perspective. I wasn't raised with a silver spoon in my mouth. I had to earn everything I ever got and usually things didn't come easy. I've worked roofing houses in the San Fernando Valley in the summertime, dug holes for street light installations, and been unemployed more than once. I know what it's like to have to scratch and claw for everything I really wanted in life. Fortunately I have always had an intellectual curiosity and quest for knowledge. I want to learn from my mistakes so I won't make them again or at least not as often. I'm vanilla, steady, stable, and consistent but I also love a challenge and have a fierce competitive nature.

Even the player with the best Process has to understand when to *Throw caution to the wind.* The game requires consistency, patience, and repetition to be successful but it also demands that you challenge yourself.

Every once in a while you must take a chance. You can't achieve great success and reach the highest highs without being willing to lose everything. You must challenge yourself daily and at least once in every round try to hit a shot that might scare you a bit.

This doesn't mean I want you to deviate from your strategy but you need to know when to take a chance. If Columbus never took a chance, America probably wouldn't have been discovered...for another few year at least.

Again, I'm not saying be careless or reckless. What I am saying is at the appropriate moment in the round, try to hit a scary flop shot over a bunker to a tucked pin. Go ahead and risk leaving it in the sand, instead of just playing safe and hitting a shot 20 feet past the hole to insure you don't make worse than a bogey. Cut the corner of a dogleg or go for the green in two on a 5 par, even if it requires flying it over a hazard to do it.

Here's what you'll learn. Either you'll pull off an amazing shot and feel proud of the fact that not only did you pull off the great shot but that you had the guts to take a chance. Or you'll dump it in the sand or hazard and if that happens, again feel proud that you took the chance and you'll learn how the ball reacted with that particular shot so that in the future you'll approach it differently. The fact that you took a chance shows that you are courageous and willing to face your demons without fear. Eventually there will be a time when you'll have to try the challenging shot to win a tournament. If you never take a chance, you'll be unprepared when the moment arises.

I hear you thinking "Wait a second, I'm confused. Do I plod along and be vanilla or should I be a risk taker?" The simple answer is, be both but be smart. You can use the rule of 1000 to help you through some of your decisions but once in a while we have to push our limits, otherwise how will we know where our limits lie.

Vanilla is so much more powerful than you can imagine. When the world is seemingly crashing down all around us, it's the calmest, steadiest, and most reliable person who appears to be the strongest.

In golf though, even the strongest and most consistent golfer can get get lost in the mundane. Golf being a marathon, can get monotonous at times. Taking an occasional risk at the appropriate time can break the monotony, test your limits, and aid your creativity.

We all know that if we are one shot back with one hole to go, we will have to risk it all to make up that shot. The *trick* is to know when it's time to take a chance when the situation isn't so obvious. I'll be honest, if you're not willing to take risks in this game, you probably won't win much. Conversely, if you take too many or unwise risks you won't win much either.

With the Process, you will develop a wisdom that will guide you through risk/reward situations and give you the confidence in the choices you make. If you are going to take a risk, you better be 100% confident it's the right decision and that's one of the biggest benefits of the Process, a strong belief system.

TRUST

I talk a lot about *belief* throughout this book. If you don't believe in yourself and what you are doing, why would you bother doing it in the first place. As I just wrote, The Process aids in developing a strong belief system.

Trust is essential for success in anything we do in life but with the complexity of the game of golf, the need to trust yourself is amplified.

That's why I say that before you hit any shot, the last thing you do is ask yourself if you're ready. What this means is, do you first, trust that what you are about to do is the correct way to proceed and second, trust your ability to execute the shot?

There really are so many factors that come into play on any one shot that it can be challenging to trust every aspect. Even with a relatively simple 10 foot putt, the pace of the greens, the slope, the grain, your stroke, the situation, and your nerves all play a factor in trusting yourself.

Again, by following the Process all these factors get simplified by your routine. You will have a sense of feel for the pace because you've walked off the distance and read the break. You see which way the grain is growing and you've worked hard on your putting stroke. The situation is unimportant as you are in the moment and focused on the task at hand and your nerves are under control because of all the work you've put in on your mental game via the Process.

Yet you still stand over the 10 footer and wonder, "Have I really read this putt correctly?"

First of all, if that thought creeps into your head, step back and start your routine over again. Assess the read of the putt to the best of your ability, pick a spot to aim yourself at, see the line in your mind and here is the most important part, TRUST yourself and pull the trigger with confidence.

This statement might not make perfect sense to you now, but I always say "It's better to miss read a putt but believe you've read it perfectly, than to read a putt perfectly but not be sure if you have." The reason being is that if you believe in your read, you'll at least make a good positive stroke and the ball will have a true roll, and maybe even go in.

If you aren't sure of your read, even if it's the right one, your uncertainty will make you put on a tentative stroke and usually come up short or start it off your line anyway. This works basically for every shot in golf. There is a direct correlation between the trust you have in yourself and the outcome of any given shot.

Things in the game of golf rarely happen by accident or at least they shouldn't. Preparation, patience, focus, acceptance, and trust are all keys to success. None of these essential attributes happen by accident and are always the byproduct of proper training and hard work.

There is another tool important to building trust in your golf game, and that's your caddy. If you want to pursue the game of golf at the highest level, a great caddy can make a huge difference. I've had so many different types of caddies throughout my career that I could write a book just about these unusual characters.

They are a rare breed. The professional caddie travels like a nomad from event to event in hopes that their player will have a breakthrough win or that the winner they are caddying for can tolerate them long enough for them to enjoy the spoils that go along with looping for a winner.

A good caddy is more than someone who carries your bag. They are equal parts, teammate, psychologist, friend, whipping boy, and cheerleader. The most important thing a caddy does though is instill trust in his player. To have an extra confirmation that what you're about to do is the right choice, can make all the difference in the world. Usually what the player asks of their caddy is "Show up, keep up, and shut up!", but some players require so much more from their caddy.

I have lots of great caddy stories but the one that represents the importance of trust happened in the first tournament I played on the South American PGA Tour in 2001 which was held in Caracas, Venezuela.

I spoke a little Spanish and used that to ask the local caddy master for the best caddy he had available. He sent out Armando, a 34 year old athletic looking man who couldn't speak a word of English and had been a caddy at the club for 15 years.

I usually don't rely too much on a caddy's advice, as I have a strong Process and belief in myself, but in the practice round I asked Armando to read a few putts. He was spot on with every read. I was such a good putter at the time that if you told me where to hit a putt and it was the right read, the ball usually went in the hole.

In the first round of the tournament I notice Armando making funny sounds and faces, and looking agitated with some of my *less than perfect* shots. This was taboo for me. I don't need a cheerleader but I certainly don't want someone who doesn't have the same trust in my game that I have. I wanted Armando to fully understand what I was about to say, so I asked my playing partner who spoke perfect English and Spanish to tell him specific instructions. If he showed any negative emotions at all about any of my poor shots, he could walk away without pay and I'd carry my own bag. He turned white as a ghost and said that he meant no offense, but he was gambling with the other caddies on every shot and losing money on me, as I was 3 over par through nine holes.

I tried to keep from laughing (as that was hilarious to me) and told him keep betting on me and not to worry. I assured him he had a great player's bag on his shoulders, just no more emotional expressions, please.

I went on to shoot 4 under par the final nine holes to end up with a round of 1 under par 70. Armando read every putt perfectly for the entire tournament and I never putted so well. I went on to finished in 4th place and made about $8,000 dollars (paid in cash!).

The trust that I had for Armando's green reading and his knowledge of the course was an important reason for my high finish and garnered him a large tip for the week. In fact I stopped reading putts and just asked him to tell me where to hit every putt. I have never done that in a tournament but that's how important trust is, whether it be in yourself or someone else.

Chapter 5

(OFF) COURSE MANAGEMENT:
The Maintenance of the Process

I've dedicated the majority of the book to what it takes to be successful on the course. Pre-Shot routine, acceptance, and focus are the attributes that are mandatory to be successful playing the game of golf. To be successful in the world of golf though, you'll need a similarly disciplined off-course regiment.

Successful people rise to the tops of their professions because they not only go to work and do their jobs exceptionally well, but they maintain exceptional daily routines.

Discipline and will are a necessity but only if they are attached to proper habits. My college golf coach used to tell me that "Practice doesn't make perfect, perfect practice makes perfect!".

If you're disciplined at eating fast food and polishing off a six-pack of beer every night, you'll probably need an unmatched amount of talent to succeed. I would recommend another path to success.

In this segment of the book, I'll go into detail as to what it takes to set yourself up for the best chance to succeed in golf away from the course, and how to avoid the common pitfalls you'll most likely come up against.

With all the work you've done to develop a strong Process and with proper off-course discipline and preparation, you'll position yourself for the absolute best chance to succeed.

Golf is a microcosm of life. How we behave in life is how we will behave on the course. You can't expect to be one way off the course and then magically transform yourself into a different person on the course. One of my all time favorite sayings is "Wherever you go, there you are". What this means is that there is no escape from your perceived problems or yourself.

You have to face life with courage, pride, and dignity. It's important to develop and incorporate a healthy lifestyle, good habits, a positive belief system, consistent daily routines, and to be nice to yourself and others. Whether you are aware of it or not, how you deal with others is most likely how you'll treat yourself.

The best way to treat others well is to learn how to love yourself. By loving yourself, I don't mean be an egotistical, narcissistic jerk. I mean learn to be forgiving, patient, kind, and to get to know and like yourself.

I know that learning to love yourself sounds corny but there was a point in my life when I had to do some serious soul searching. I didn't like what I saw when I looked in the mirror and I was profoundly unhappy. The moment I decided to change my life for the better, the first thing I did was to try to get to know myself. It was a deep and sometimes painful examination of what led me to the decisions I had made and what caused me to continuously think the way I would in any given moment.

I had to look back on some of the key moments in my life and decide what led me to that point and why I choose to say or behave the way I did in those particular situations.

You might be surprised by what you'll find if you take a fearless look at what makes you tick. I know it surprised me. Most of us spend our entire lives hiding from what we really are for fear that when we find out, it won't be pretty. The thing is though, if you don't ever *find yourself* you'll probably continue to make the same mistakes your entire life.

The Process will work for anyone but it works quicker with the cleanest slate possible. That's why it's so much easier for me to start with younger players. They haven't been corrupted by the perceived negativity that the world has to offer.

As we get older and grow more cynical, our minds seem to see more negativity around us than we did in our youth. This doesn't mean that as we get to a certain age, we reach a point of no return. It just requires more work to change our character and personality the older and more set in our ways we become. The more we have on our chalkboard of life, the longer it will take to clean the slate, so to speak.

The beautiful thing is that with a fearless search of who you are, a proper disciplined daily routine, and the development of a strong Process you can achieve goals that would have never been attainable to you before.

FITNESS AND NUTRITION

For those of you with a very disciplined fitness and nutritional regiment, good for you. Keep up the good work! For the other 99.9% of us, let's get started on the simplest way to make an immediate change for the better in our lives, *Fitness and Nutrition.*

First of all, it's important to know that perfection isn't the goal, only to constantly make strides in the right direction which lead to an all around healthier lifestyle. If we begin with baby steps, it will become so much easier to reach and sustain a full sprint then if we try to change our habits too quickly.

I have been a competitive athlete my entire life. I know what it takes to train my body for peak performance. I worked as a health club manager/salesman/trainer in my early 20's. It was there that I truly began a lifelong love affair with exercise, fitness, and nutrition.

I would work out religiously with a three days on and one day off routine for four straight years. I was 6'4" and 225 lbs. with a 6% body fat ratio. I could do amazing things such as, 1000 inverted sit-ups at one sitting, bench press 325 lbs., and play A-level racquetball for two hours without a break.

As a manager and salesman, my honest enthusiasm for fitness was a helpful enticement for potential sales. People would come in and I would tell them that "You've made the best decision of your life by coming in today", and I meant it because I truly wanted to help people become the best they could be. Which I guess is what made me a great salesman. I really loved fitness and helping people to achieve their own fitness goals.

I spoke earlier in the book about how Tiger Woods changed the game of golf and how he became the new prototypical golfer of today's game. Beyond his amazing golfing talents, it was his physical fitness that differentiated him from other golfers.

Other tour players looked at him and thought "If I ever want to compete with that guy, I better get my ass in the gym!" and that's exactly what the modern day player has done. A lot of people believe the reason players are hitting the ball so far is the equipment. That's partly true but the modern player is so much fitter, more athletic, and stronger than the player of my youth.

Advancements in fitness training methods have improved as fast as the equipment technology. These advancements have led to bigger, stronger, quicker, and more flexible players but just as importantly, it has given the modern player the stamina to endure a grueling golf season.
Here is a funny story that illustrates the importance of stamina and just how physically and mentally exhausting golf can be.

Years ago I played in a mini-tour tournament at least once a week for years. In one of these tournaments, I saw a friend of mine Patrick who I hadn't seen in a while. He was a great golfer and had qualified to play on the Australian Tour. I jokingly asked him what he was doing playing with us nobody's. He said he was just happy to be home and playing with his friends.
It was a one day tourney and I shot 66 to win and was in an obviously good mood after the round. Patrick shot 77 and hacked it around miserably all over a relatively easy golf course.
I joked with him after the round, "What have those damn Aussie done to your game?!?!". He said he was completely and utterly exhausted and that he had just played in nine tournaments in a row. I laughed and said I've played in fifty tournaments in a row!

He threw me a wry smile and said it wasn't the same thing to be living at home and traveling less than an hour to play one or two day tournaments. Traveling every week to different parts of a foreign country playing four day tournaments for nine straight weeks without a break is exhausting.

I called him a baby and rubbed the winners check in his face and told him a little fatigue was no excuse (that's how pro golfers lovingly treat each other!).

He told me, and I'll never forgot this, "If you're lucky and keep playing well, you'll find out what I mean some day".

A few years after that encounter with Patrick, I qualified for the Nike Tour in 1998. My first real stint out on the tour was a six week stretch through the southern part of the USA at the beginning of summer. It was unbearably hot and humid every day.

Between practicing, practice rounds, and tournament play in that hot weather, professional golf turned out to be an amazingly tiring life choice. In every round of golf you are walking at least four miles and doing so under relatively stressful mental conditions.

By the sixth week out, I was so mentally and physically drained I could barely get out of bed and probably wasn't making much sense in any conversation.

I played that last tournament so poorly that I didn't particularly care that I had missed the cut. In fact I was just relieved that I would be getting home to see my daughter and rest up for a week. Coincidentally one of the first persons I saw when I got back to California was Patrick. I reminded him of the conversation we had years before and I apologized for my idiotic comments to him. I then understood exactly what he was talking about and I learned that to be competitive as a pro, I would have to get more disciplined with my fitness and nutrition regiment, which I did.

I could go into detail about all the different training programs that would help increase your stamina, flexibility, strength, and speed but that's not for me to dictate in this book, maybe that will be in my next book. What I'm here to tell you is that you need to find something and stick to it, whatever it might be. With my students I give suggestions as to what might work best for them to train their bodies for the daily grind of tour golf. I'll just tell you that self-discipline is incredibly important if you want to achieve success in this game. There are many good books and websites for golf fitness training and I recommend doing research to find something that looks interesting, useful, and best suited for your specific needs.

To go along with your training, you'll need a healthy nutritional diet to help sustain your stamina and focus throughout a golf season. Your body is like an engine. If you don't feed it the right fuel, your engine will run poorly and eventually breakdown.

Junk food and soda might be a quick, easy, and an inexpensive meal but in the long run it will eventually cause you any number of health problems. I also believe that just the act of buying that junk shows little will or discipline. Do your research and find a proper diet.

Five years ago I stopped eating meat "cold turkey", no pun intended! The food I was eating made me lethargic and I would often get sick to my stomach from eating meat.

This isn't the part of the book where I start telling you all the social ills about why you shouldn't eat meat.

I'm no hypocrite, I ate meat for the first 40+ years of my life, so no judgements here. I'll just say that you might want to read up on the subject and see if a vegetarian diet might work for you. I can say that I have lost 20 lbs and kept that weight off for these five years and I haven't had so much as an upset stomach in that time.

Again, I could go on and on about all the diets you could try but that's up to you to find out what works best. Beyond being a vegetarian, I have cut out gluton in my diet, lowered my carb intake and have experimented with juice fasting and whole raw foods. I recently saw a documentary film that inspired me to try something new and I highly recommend you look into it.

The film is called "Fat, Sick, and Nearly Dead" by Joe Cross. He is a young successful Australian businessman and it's a film about his own battle with his weight and the disease brought on by his admittedly awful diet. Besides being really well made and informative, the documentary is a really touching and inspiring movie. Learn more about it at www.fatsickandnearlydead.com.

Another great documentary I would recommended you watch on this subject of diet is called "Forks over Knives". This film goes into detail about how most of our illnesses and diseases are caused by what we eat. See www.forksoverknives.com.

Just like with a training regiment, it's essential that a proper diet be part of your off-course Process. Whatever diet you might choose, make sure it's healthy, nutritional, and you have the discipline to stick with it.

TIME MANAGEMENT

Beyond fitness and diet, there is another tool at your disposal to assist you with the rigors of professional golf, *time management*. I've talked about the importance of repetition and routines but organization can be just as crucial to a players success.

Some people seem to be born with the gift of organization. In fact there is a mental disorder know as OCD or *obsessive compulsive disorder* which compels those with the affliction to micro-organize every facet of their lives. I wouldn't suggest having a level of organization that borders on compulsion but I would recommend managing your time more effectively.

There are only so many hours in a day and the life of a golfer has many demands. I spoke briefly of the typical week in the life of a professional golfer but let me again give you an idea of the time demands. The average PGA Tour player enters about 25 tournaments a year. That is 25 weeks of basically the same routine. Monday and Tuesday practice rounds, followed by practice, Pro-Ams or rest on Wednesday. Thursday through Sunday are tournament rounds if you're playing well enough to make cuts and play the weekend that is. And don't forget travel to and from events.

There may be additional demands for time from autograph seeking fans, media interviews, sponsor or endorser events, and friends and family. All of these demands leave very little time for your own personal entertainment or even relaxation.

Some would say that golf is enough entertainment and relaxation, so why would a golfer need more. If you are fortunate enough to become a professional golfer, you'll see in time that it is a very demanding profession. Sure it's one of the best professions in the world but you have to go into it knowing that to be successful you must be ready for hard work. Learning time management will help to keep your life stable, calm, and remove that constant hectic disorderly feeling possessed by the disorganized player.

Each day you should take a few minutes to put down in your calendar as specifically as possible what you intend to accomplish and when you want to do it. Plans change regularly throughout the day but if you have an idea of what your agenda is and put it down in writing, you'll have the flexibility to adjust to changes.

Just as with a golf shot, you want to have intentions for your daily schedule, not expectations that all will go exactly as planned. If you get attached to your set schedule and something goes wrong or changes it can cause a disruption in your flow.

You will find that in time your morning agendas will closely match what you actually accomplished for the day. It takes experience but if you really are consistent with your daily planning it makes it so much easier to achieve your goals. Remember, proper preparation is mandatory for success and having an organized plan is part of that preparation, whether it be on or off the course.

With today's technology, the need to carry around a large schedule book or organizer is unnecessary. Today's cell phones in the palm of your hands is all you'll need. You can place everything required of your time for the day on that cell phone calendar and carry that with you wherever you go. Sorry but there are no more excuses for being disorganized. Today's collegiate players have the same issues. Between their studies (which should always be no.1 priority), golf schedule, and a social life, a college golfer has to handle a full schedule.

Surprisingly though, college athletes are usually more organized than the average professional because their schedules are pretty much already set up for them. They have set class schedules, mandated practices, and play schedules set up by their coaches, and if they get all of their studying in, maybe they have time for a friend or the occasional party. The main thing for the college golfer to consider is, "What are my priorities?".

RELATIONSHIPS

The life of a golfer can be a lonely one. In my fourteen years as professional golfer, I have traveled to 25 different countries and most all of the

50 United States. The travel was one of the best parts of my golfing experience, but it took me away from home at least 25 weeks of every year.

The hotels all start to look alike. In fact I remember waking up alone in a hotel after a long road trip and being so confused that I had to call the front desk to ask what city I was in. Honestly, for $100 I couldn't have told you where I was. It's a funny story but it illustrates how monotonous and disorienting life on the road can be.

The friendships I made along the way were priceless. Golfers are a rare and unusual breed. I think my next book will be about all the crazy characters I encountered in all my years as a competitive golfer.

Golfers are a thrifty lot as well. It's very common for players to buddy up on the road to cut costs, so you get to learn a lot about these guys. A good roommate can be like a good teammate. They can help you out in times of need, and we all can use a little help on the road.

One of my best friends on the road was a player from Sweden named Marcus. He was one of the funniest guys I ever knew but apparently this Swede didn't like to wear socks. His feet stunk so bad that I used to have to travel with a can of air freshener! He was though, a friend I could really rely on and made life fun on the road when I very much missed my friends and family back home.

It's important who you choose to share expenses with and who you'll room with. Make sure they are a positive person and heading in the same direction with their own Process. Be sure to let them know that you have specific goals and require quiet time to read and work on your meditation techniques. If they have a problem with your practice of the Process, wish them luck and move on until you find someone you bond with. You may not want to room with anyone at all. I would suggest trying both and see which way works best for you. Eventually, when you are making millions of dollars on Tour this will be a moot point, as expenses aren't as big of an issue.

The most important relationship for a golfer is the one with the opposite sex or same sex if that's what you prefer. It's really difficult for anyone to find that special person to share their life with but for a golfer there are more than the usual obstacles.

The time constraints, long hours, and extended road trips away from each other are only the tip of the iceberg of the possible land mines awaiting a golfer's relationship.

A golfer struggles everyday with the daily grind and pressures associated with succeeding in this game. The strong support of anyone involved in your life is essential. A relationship can make or break a golfer. Get involved with the right person and it could make all the difference in your career, but get involved with the wrong person and your success potential drops rapidly.

I spoke earlier in the book about my marriage and how I allowed it to nearly ruin my career. I heard "When are you going to get a real job?" a hundred times and I couldn't take it any more. I needed to feel that the person I was with had my back. I didn't need a cheerleader, just someone who understood that I loved what I did and gave me the support to chase my dream.

I'm obviously not going to tell you who to be in a relationship with or even if you should be in one. I will say this though, make sure that whomever you choose to be with, it's mandatory that they support you 100%.

Golf is the most mentally challenging sport in the world and it's essential that we make things as easy as possible. The love and support of the person we care most about may be the difference that pushes you over the top.

There is another side of this story though.

Remember that guy named Tiger Woods? I saw him up close in 2000 at the US Open and I was convinced that the only way anyone would ever consistently beat him was if he got injured or married.

Tiger's woes are well documented and I won't go into his sad personal story but I will say this, he should have never gotten married! He is a wolf and there is nothing wrong with that as long as you're honest with yourself and the person you're with. Tiger got married and because he is a wolf, he couldn't stay faithful. He got caught and his life has been in a tailspin ever since. It's my opinion that being a wolf, Tiger's mistake as a golfer wasn't so much the cheating but getting married.

Let me be absolutely clear, cheating is WRONG but trying to be something you're not is almost as destructive to your psyche.

He wasn't honest with himself and more importantly, he wasn't honest with his wife Elin and that wasn't fair to her.

We each need to be honest with ourselves and those we choose to have in our lives. It's the fairest and most decent thing to do for both parties involved. Besides, you're a golfer and by definition a difficult person to deal with, so don't make matters worse by being dishonest.

So if you feel the need to find someone special, go for it but choose wisely. Otherwise there is nothing wrong with being alone. Once you qualify for the PGA Tour, you will really have to be careful about who you choose to be with. You will be headed for a life in the fast lane with a lot of potential to earn millions of dollars and impending suitors will coincidentally be knocking down your door.

Be leery of the gold diggers but don't become cynical. If you are true to yourself, treat people as you would want them to treat you, and follow the Process, you'll recognize the phony from the real and all good things will come to you in time. As for women, don't worry you'll be fine, as you seem to have a much better grasp on the whole relationship thing than men do!

BE THE SAME PERSON ON AND OFF THE COURSE

There was a time in my life when I was a totally different person than I am now. Usually we all grow up and mature with age but I mean I was *another* person. I grew up like most kids thirsting for attention. I discovered early on that people paid more attention to you if you were the best at what you were doing.

I was a gifted athlete and my need for attention drove me to be a *win at all costs* character. This character produced two things. First, it made me work harder than anyone else to be the best and second, I lost a lot of friends.

Turns out people don't like it when you try intensely to beat them all the time. I found out that not everyone possesses the burning desire to win that I have. Most people just want to have fun, but I couldn't have fun unless I won.

Soon I began to develop an attitude. I resented those who didn't have the will to win and resented those who resented my will to win even more. This pushed me further away from those who couldn't keep up and narrowed the list of friends I had.

In high school this attitude grew stronger because I moved to a new community and needed to establish myself. I played sports but had problems with coaches and teammates, because I felt they lacked my desire to win.

I loved golf because this was a sport in which I had no one to blame but myself. In a sense it brought me a certain peace, but I also turned the intensity that had been once been directed towards others upon myself. I became my harshest critic and that led to the further developing of my aggressive attitude.

My battle with inner demons, a 30 year development of some really bad habits, and poor personality traits led me to a critical fork in the road. I found myself walking down a dark path when I reached a point to which I couldn't just keep going forward, I had to make a critical decision in my life. I was married, I had a beautiful two year old daughter, a decent job teaching golf, and a budding professional golf career. From the outside you might have thought I was very happy and that I was nowhere near rock bottom. The truth was, I was miserable.

I had little patience and felt that I had no support, which made me resentful. I felt that if I was going to be made unhappy I would give the same in return. I was so unaware of the destruction I was causing in my life and my families life that I just started feel numb about everything.

I was so unhappy that I couldn't take it any more. So there I was at that proverbial fork in the road and I had to make a choice. Take a left down the *Road of Self Pity* and eventually get to a point of no return with my misery or take a right up the *Road to Enlightenment,* a place where all things are possible.

Sounds like such an easy choice, right? Let me tell you that this was the toughest decision I ever made in my life. My father used to tell me that "It's easy to quit, anyone can do it, but to persevere in the face of adversity takes real courage". I finally understood what he meant.

To go down the road of self pity would have been easy. That road required no change, just keep heading in the same negative direction enjoying my misery. The road to enlightenment is a long difficult soul cleansing journey which requires a sometimes painful look deep into who we are and what caused us to arrive at the fork in the road in the first place.

I remember the day vividly when I made the tough decision to make a change in my life. I was with a good friend after a poor round of golf and he looked at me and asked "Are you happy?" knowing full well that I wasn't.

I don't think anyone had actually seriously asked me that question because I was kind of stunned to hear it. I was in a particularly bad mood and snapped back "What the fuck do you think?". He smiled and said "I can show you a way to find peace in your life", and here is the craziest thing, I said a little less sarcastically than usual, "Ok, what's this ray of sunshine you've got for me?".

He asked if I was serious about learning what he had to say and amazingly, I said yes. I had reached such a point of utter desperation that I was going down for the third count and I felt that someone had just thrown me a life preserver.

We began the next day. He sat me down and talked for about three hours about what he had found in his life that made him happy. Not a cult or religion but a solid foundation for how to think and behave basically based on what is truly important in life, inner peace.

I listened intently without speaking a word and when it was finally my turn to speak, I metaphorically vomited out 34 years of crap locked inside of me which just spewed out all over the floor. It felt really good to get all that crap out of my system and out into the open.

It was from that moment that I decided to go on a long journey to find a path to, for lack of a better word, *Enlightenment.* It was then that I began reading everything I could get my hands on and I watched very little TV for about three years.

Through this journey I began to developed what I call "The Process" and the basic fundamentals of this book.

One of the most important things I learned on my journey was to be the same person on *and* off the course. I remember driving to golf tournaments like a maniac in a rage. Impatiently weaving in and out of drivers that had no idea how to drive (I mean the nerve of them getting in MY way).

In a supermarket I was aloof to anyone, barely even acknowledging their existence, just going about my business. With my daughter I was a patient and loving father. On the golf course I was a calm and confident competitor. A different person in every different situation, or so I thought. What I was really, was the same person in every situation.

I would drive like a maniac to tournaments and once I arrived at the course I would say "Ok now I'm the calm and confident golfer". But the first time something went wrong on the course I became the same impatient maniac as I was behind the wheel. With my daughter, I was the loving patient father until she wouldn't stop crying or wouldn't eat her food. It was then that I would get frustrated and very impatient with her, even trying to *reason* with an infant.

I had to become the same person wherever I was or whatever I was doing, so I could truly become the calm and confident person I so desperately wanted to be.

I began by researching philosophers, psychologists, and even some spiritual leaders theories of happiness and inner peace. What I discovered was a common thread that was similar to all great thinkers underlying in all their beliefs.

Be good to yourself and to others. Don't steal, lie, cheat, kill, or in any way harm yourself or another. Every religion or great thinker relates the same sort of top ten ideals. It's after those obvious principles where they begin to differ and in my opinion become inconsequential, such as which land is holier, what direction to pray, etc.

I used the principle philosophies of everything I studied to develop the Process and over the past 14 years I have been refining it into what you are reading now.

ACT AS IF...

A few years into the beginning of my *quest for knowledge,* a good friend of mine knew I was absorbing every philosophical lesson I could get my hands on. He introduced me to something he thought I might find interesting. It was a CD by a motivational speaker named Tony Robbins.

It wasn't anything I hadn't heard before but there was something I found absolutely fascinating. Most of the CD was motivational rah rah stuff and some solid organizational principles which are really useful but the part that changed my life in a way was a theory he called *Act as if*.

The way he described it, *Act as if* simply means that if you want to be the best golfer in the world for example, wake up in the morning and drink your coffee as if you're the best golfer. Brush your teeth as if you're the best golfer in the world, read the newspaper as if your the best golfer in the world, etc. No matter what you're doing, proceed as if you're the best and you'll soon begin to believe you are.

Here is how this simple strategy changed my game and ultimately my career. I was always a pretty good putter but it always seemed to me that other guys were making more putts than I was (but don't we all feel that way). I worked hard on my putting daily but all that did was make me a consistently *good* putter. Good putter don't win major tournaments, exceptional putters do.

No matter how hard I worked on my putting I just couldn't get over the hump. My mechanics were fundamentally sound but I just couldn't consistently make enough putts and I believe it was because of my mental approach.

After listening to Mr. Robbins CD I decided to give it a try. From the minute I turned off the the CD I began to *Act as if* I was the greatest putter in the world. Some psychologists say that if you lie to yourself long enough about a particular subject, eventually you'll begin to actually believe the lie as the truth.

This is exactly what began to happen when I acted as if I was the greatest putter in the world. I told myself a hundred times a day that I was the greatest putter in the world.

I used to practice putting at a nearby driving range with a beautiful putting green which had lots of local gamblers who weren't afraid to putt anyone for any amount of money. They all knew me and knew that I could putt but that didn't stop them from inviting me into their money games. I always held my own and probably made more than I lost but I wasn't nearly as dominant as I should have been.

Since I was now acting as if I was the best putter in the world, I thought I would do them a favor and tell them that they should save their money. I told them not invite me into their game, because "I was the best putter in the world" and would undoubtedly take all their cash from them.

This attitude would only make them want to gamble with me even more. They would laugh and say "We love beating the best putter in the world!" That turned out to be a costly mistake on their part.

It was amazing how quickly my putting improved, and people started to take notice. I had a hard time getting anyone to gamble with me because I was so hard to beat. The more I told myself and anyone else who would listen that I was the best putter in the world, the more I started to believe it and I mean REALLY believe it.

My friends were growing tired of me always telling them that "I was the best putter in the world!" but I didn't care. The more I said it, the more it sank in, and the better I putted.

Eventually after a few months, I got to the point where I didn't need to say it at all anymore because it was becoming apparent for all to see. There was a point in my career that it seemed like I would make every putt inside of ten feet and would make a few putts over ten feet in every round. It was at this time that I realized that though mechanics and alignment are important to good putting, they are rendered virtually useless without having a strong belief system established in your subconscious.

You can have the best mechanics and align yourself perfectly but if you don't believe you'll make putts, to put it simply, you won't.

It takes time to change your belief system so that it becomes deeply ingrained in your subconscious and you'll need the assistance of the Process and tools like *Act as if* to help replace self doubts with true belief.

Here is another important point illustrated by a short story.

I played in a two day tournament at the peak of my Act as if experiment. I was paired with a friend of mine who I hadn't seen in a while. He noticed a demonstrative change in my attitude for the better and he asked what it was that I was doing differently.

I explained some of the changes I had made in my life and how happy I was with Process and all the work I had put into it.

I didn't tell him about my Act as if experiment but of course I told him that I was now the greatest putter in the world. He looked at me funny and we went out to play the first round.

I played well but didn't have one putt go in the hole from outside five feet. We walked off the 18th green and he smiled and said "Thought you were the best putter in the world? You didn't make a thing!" he said with a chuckle.

What I told him was that I had made every putt I looked at today. The smile turned to a confused look and he asked what I meant. I told him that it was my intention to make every putt and in my mind I had. I hit every single putt that round on the exact line with the exact speed I thought I needed to make the putt. There is nothing more you can do than that, so consider it a make if you do that. The course was unfamiliar to me so I didn't know the greens well and my reads were just off. I assured him that tomorrow would be a different story, because as long as I am doing exactly what I intend to do, it's only a matter of time before the putts start to fall.

To put it another way, if you hit every shot solidly and directly at the flag and a big gust of wind came up after you made contact and blew the ball into the sand, would that make you a poor iron player? Of course not, you're doing exactly what you intended and after that you're at he mercy of golf's intangibles.

The next day I made almost every putt, shot 65, won the two day tourney and converted another believer to the way of the Process.

I ran into my friend a few years later and he told me that he never forgot what we talked about that day and how it had changed his attitude towards putting for the better.

He, like most, felt that success was determined by the outcome and not the Process.

Through the strengthening of my Process, the need to *Act as if* became unnecessary because I really did believe I was the best putter in the world. That way of thinking became the truth, not an act.
It probably took about two years before the act completely become the truth, but when it did I could

stand over any putt and believe that I could stroke the putt exactly as needed.

Once you know you can confidently stroke a putt under any circumstances, there will be no need to act. That's the beauty of *Act as if*, it is one of the easier ways to alter your subconscious.

Enough conscious positive reinforcement will have a positive effect on your subconscious and once the belief is in the subconscious there is no need to act. I wasn't acting anymore, in my mind I truly was the best putter in the world.

The funny thing is that *Act as if* worked so well that maybe I should have acted as if I was the best golfer in the world instead of just the best putter.

SWING MECHANICS: NECESSITY OR TRAP?

I turned professional in 1989 and began working as an instructor for a public course in Los Angeles.

After six months I was giving 50 half hour lessons a week and probably could have given a lot more if I cared to.

After only a year at that course I moved to a nearby course and became director of golf instruction for six years. In that time I would say that I had given more than 5,000 golf lessons and at least 4,000 of those were solely on the golf swing.

It seemed that all anyone wanted to learn was how to hit the ball farther. No matter how much I stressed the importance of the short game or putting, it was as if people were fixated on their swings.

I had a long time student who would come once a week for years. He refused to learn any other part of the game, all he wanted to do was perfect his swing mechanics. Every time he would show up I would say the same stupid joke, "Today's the day we work on your short game, right?". I knew the answer was always going to be "No" but it was funny to me just to ask.

It got so bad with some of my students that I began to mandate that any new students I took on who bought a series of six lessons had to use one of the lessons for the short game or putting.

When I began playing tournament golf I realized that it wasn't just my students or the average weekend golfer who was fixated on their swing, it was the professional as well. I would observe some talented players spending countless hours on the range working on swings that even to the trained eye looked technically sound.

I'll say something that might ruffle the feathers of my fellow golf instructors, I never took an official golf lesson in my life and never really understood why people work so hard on their swings. Granted, this is one of the most complicated of all sports and it is essential to learn the game properly but I feel that constant work on the swing takes away from the goal of the game, hitting the ball at your target.

I read a book a long time ago called "I Found the Golf God" which was written by Dori O'Rourke an instructor and follower of Chuck Hogan. Chuck Hogan was an instructor who's main theory was "Target Golf". To put it simply he believed that the more you put your focus on the target the better your chances of hitting it were.

"I Found the Golf God" told a story of a man who through a chain of coincidences had the opportunity to learn under the guidance of a wise guru. One of the lessons the guru teaches the man is how mechanics can get in the way of the goal.

He tells the man to walk 50 yards over to a large pine tree, touch the tree and walk back. The man does as he's asked and returns. This time the guru instructs the man to again touch the tree but now to focus on how he is walking. "I want you to notice everything that is happening with your body, how your ankles and knees flex and straighten. The way your muscles are contracting, how your arms swing, and what causes the motion of their swinging". The man takes to this task awkwardly, trying to think of everything that is going on mechanically with his body. He meanders around and even begins to have fun with the exercise. Just when he believes he has figured out what makes his body work, he walks back to the guru and proclaims "I got it!". The guru asks, "Got What? You didn't do as I asked." Baffled the man asks, "What do you mean? I figured out how my body works when I walk." The guru says "That's nice but I asked you to walk over and touch the tree and you never even got close to it." The moral of the story is that we spend so much time focusing on what makes our bodies work and how to hit the perfect golf shot that we lose focus of the most important thing, our target.

Again, let me state that I do believe that swing mechanics are important and every great golfer including myself works diligently on our swing. The important thing I'm saying is that once you've got the swing that works, go with it and stop the constant tinkering. It's ok to do occasional maintenance on your swing to make sure it's doing what you want it to, but don't obsess over it.

I have a straight ball flight and don't draw or fade the ball unless I have to. I know my swing so well that when something goes wrong I know it's one of two things. Either my shoulders move too fast on the downswing which causes me to get ahead of my release point and I hit a fade or block to the right. Or I don't turn enough in my backswing and come over the top and hit a pull or hook to the left which rarely happens. When you have an understanding like this of your swing, you shouldn't make too many changes. Try to keep it as simple as possible, because the more you make changes the less sure you are of what went wrong with imperfect shots. There is a long list of great players, some of whom have even won major championships, who felt they needed to make changes to their swings to stay on top. Hal Sutton is the best example of this obsession with swing mechanics. Sutton was a dominant player in the early 80's winning 15 times on the PGA Tour including a PGA Championship and then he decided to change his swing.

Ten years of struggling to find the one magical swing with no results and nearly losing his tour status, he finally decided to give up and just hit the ball. He stopped thinking about his swing and decided to just have fun and play golf. Sutton had an amazing rebirth in golf, winning several times in the late 90's and making his way back to the Ryder Cup team in 1999 and 2002.

Padraig Harrington won the British Open in 2007 and 2008 and the PGA Championship in 2008 and was named Player of the year in 2008. Then for some unexplained reason, he went through a swing change. He hasn't been the same player since. Some things make no sense.

Tiger Woods has gone through three different big name instructors and has changed his swing every time he hires a new swing coach. I used to say that Tiger was better at what he did than any other human in history was at what they did. He came as close to perfection in a horribly complex sport as anyone ever did, and yet he still feels the need to make changes.

I heard he made some of the changes to protect his legs and back and if that's true, it's absolutely appropriate but he made those changes and still continues to change things. Tiger, you're the greatest athlete to ever compete in professional golf, please just hit the ball at your target and stop the tinkering, because it's a trap.

If you stop to think about it, when you can produce a perfectly struck golf shot that flies directly at your target with enough distance, why would you think that you couldn't do that every time with the swing you just produced. I say it's probably good enough, so make what you have work the best it can be and then work on your Process. If you're an accomplished player, it's undoubtably your poor Process which is making you hit poor shots not your swing mechanics.

I had this debate with some good players and they nearly bit my head off on this subject. The nerve of me claiming that their poor shots were caused by how they were thinking and not some minute flaw in their swing. I believe it is easier for a player to blame their swing than to actually have to do work on their Process.

It's easy, and I feel a bit lazy, for golfers to go to the range and just beat balls until they feel satisfied that *now* their swing feels better and all will work fine tomorrow, it's not. And no matter how much time you spend on swing mechanics, under pressure the same flaws will reoccur.

My college golf coach used to say "Golf swings don't hold up under pressure, golfer's do!". That's why with the proper Process and a lot of work at it, you won't need the endless hours of back breaking range work.

Whole hearted belief in your swing as it is, will carry you a long way further than constantly tinkering and believing that if you work for the perfect swing mechanics they will be there when you need them.

THE *IT FACTOR*

I have always been a very observant individual. It is a hobby of mine to people watch and I would consider myself an amateur sociologist. I find people fascinating and learn from my observations of them. If you pay close enough attention, you begin to understand what drives them to make their decisions and say the things they say.

With thirty years in the game of golf I've observed a lot of golfers and the unusual decisions they make. Another thing I've observed are the rare individuals that have the *It factor*.

These are the people who seem to have an intangible quality about them that the less observant might not see. I can spot them because I know what to look for. As a player, I encountered only five players I felt had the can't miss *It factor.* Four of these players went on to win on the PGA Tour and the other had a fluke injury that derailed his career. Generally speaking, the *It factor* golfer goes about their business a bit differently than the norm. They seem to be more organized, focused, and have a noticeable sense of purpose. The *It* golfer is seldom seen goofing off or in line at the nearest fast food restaurant. They have a presence about them that when they walk into a room they exude a certain confidence without saying a word.

Have you ever walked into a crowded party and noticed someone there that you've never seen before but you just couldn't take you're eyes off of them? Most likely, that's the *It* person.

I would define the *It factor* person as the one who possesses a *true* inner self belief. I'm not talking about the false bravado you might find at a Hollywood party, where all the inhabitants desperately need the attention and respect of those around them. They tell you how great they are when they (and you if you're observant) know that they are full of it.

A true inner self belief comes from a few places. Great parenting and a strong family can create the positive esteem required to truly believe in one's ability. Steely and unrelenting determination to become the best can create the drive required to have *It*. Possibly some are just born that way but I doubt it.

I believe the real path to having *It,* is discipline and a positive mental approach that is incorporated in their everyday life. They truly believe in what they are doing and can do it in any given moment no matter how big the situation. In fact, it's their success in big moments that makes the *It factor* noticeable to even the least observant. They are fearless and calm in the face of intense pressure.

I was once asked what makes Tiger so much better than anyone else, when he was at the peak of his career. I would tell them that he had *It*. I never met anyone who had such a presence about them. He had an aura of confidence that surrounded him. What he did have that only a rare few have ever possessed is the ability to not only perform, but consistently excel in the biggest moments. The bigger the moment the better he performed. How many brilliant shots did he pull off to win tournaments? Actually, almost too many to list. Most can hit a delicate little flop shot over sand with no green to work with, but only a select few have the courage and belief to pull that shot off on the 72nd hole of the Masters.

Every *It factor* golfer has a Process whether they know it or not. They stick to there routine and have their lives in order. I think one of the main reasons I decided to write "The Process" was to help people find the *It factor* in themselves.

The biggest misconception about *It* is that only a few gifted or fortunate people can have *It,* but that's not true. Through devotion to the Process and some hard work they can be created. It's no coincidence that the players who win are the ones with the best work ethic, confidence, and are Process oriented.

CONCLUSION

You have just read a lot of information that has taken a lifetime to compile. Thirty-plus years of blood, sweat, and tears went into this book. Every story true and every theory tried and tested in competition.

I believe that's the difference between this and most any other book on the subject of mental training and professional golf preparation. I have been involved in most every type of pressure situation at every level of the game, both as an amateur and professional.

My father was an excellent psychologist and a scratch golfer. He imparted all of his wisdom on me. However, like most golf mental trainers he never competed in any golf tournaments of note. He could only imagine what was going on in the mind of a player under intense pressure. He did have a good idea but it's just not the same thing as living it.

It's well documented that my skill level probably wasn't anywhere near that of the top players I competed against, but it was my Process that kept me competitive in professional golf for 14 years. I had the desire, tenacity, and work ethic to hang in there with anyone.

Every year I added to the Process and I believe the more time I devoted to the practice of the Process the better I got. That's the secret to improvement in the game of golf...find a Process, stick with it, and never stop learning.

Today I'm 49 years old and I still learn something about the game and myself every time I tee it up. I still look for ways to add to my Process and make my game even stronger and most likely will try my chances at qualifying for the Senior Tour. You can always get better and that's the beauty of golf, a perfect game will never be played.

As a 13 year old I was a top bowler in my age group, averaging over 200 for the year. My older brothers have both bowled perfect game 300's more than a dozen times each! I got bored of bowling for the reason that once you bowl a perfect game, where do you go next?

In dog racing they say that if the dog ever catches the rabbit he will never run as fast again because once he's caught his dream, he loses his desire.

Golf's magic number was 59 for a long time but now that feat has been accomplished several times in competition. There isn't a perfect score in golf and even if there was, no one would ever shoot it. Golfers will forever be reaching for that carrot which lies just beyond their grasp. It's the desire to chase that carrot which fuels all golfers dreams and aspirations.

It can be maddening when something we want so badly is just beyond our reach. This is why we must have a Process that enables us to enjoy the chase and to help us learn that it's not the carrot but the journey to grasp it that matters most.

I read a book on the subject of sport psychology by a rather famous author and he said his way was the *easy way* to improve your game. I make no such claim. It is incredibly difficult to succeed at golf's highest level. The amount of work required to put into your game, body, and mind is exhausting and never ending.

No way will I lie to you and tell you that this is going to be easy because it's not. Golf, being a marathon and not a sprint, may at times seem like a test of the human will. From what I've seen in my long career, competitive golf can be absolutely exhausting if you don't have the proper Process. I've seen dozens of potentially great players quit the game from extreme burn out or perceived unrelenting disappointment. Be prepared to work hard and if you faithfully follow everything I've written about in this book, the Process will give you protection from burn out. Like I said, it's not easy but the more you work the Process the easier it gets.

Once you begin to see how well it works, you start to believe in it more and the stubbornness to fight it and yourself goes away. When the stubbornness goes away you'll feel fresher and free of the fatigue caused by fighting against the flow.

I will say this though, that if you're anything like me, the work required to become a great golfer isn't really work at all. I loved the mental training and practicing the physical game. I could practice all day or at least until my back couldn't handle it anymore. Even the most difficult days of golf I would considered to be better than the best days of an office job. Plus, if you really love doing something and are good at it, how difficult could putting in the required effort really be?

Some of my students take to the Process very quickly because they are fully aware that something had to change in their life and golf game. Other students fight it, unwilling to give up the poor habits and the security blankets they have held onto their whole life.

I have 100% confidence in the Process because of how it works for me and how it has worked for every one of my students. I believe that anyone can benefit from the Process.

I am positive that if I took five players from the PGA Tour Qualifying School and taught them the Process that they would all have better and longer careers than five equal players without the Process. The Process isn't just for PGA Tour players. I work with players of all levels and all showed significant improvement. It's not magic and almost not worth bragging about, because most golfers think so poorly on the golf course. They have such bad habits in their game and their life, that any positive change would make a difference.

I love working with weekend golfers because they are usually less resistant to change. They know that they need help, have open ears and an eagerness to learn. With top players it can be a bit more challenging.

They achieved their talents through a lot of hard work and feel that they only need a tweak here or there to put them over the top, so when you tell them that their process is insufficient, they will fight to preserve their own way.

I spend a lot of time explaining to top players that there are numerous amounts of great players out there. If they want to reach the top level they must have the correct Process to guide them on a path to success. Once they apply the training of the Process, they begin to see just how poor their previous mental approach to the game had been.

I get many questions because the Process is something unusual to most players. What do you mean I can't get upset with a bad shot? Why do I need to meditate? Why do I need to have the same routine every time? Are just a few of the questions I get on a weekly basis. It's amazing how tightly we hold onto our poor habits and misguided way of thinking.

What the Process delivers is a consistent ability to handle all challenges and obstacles that might be perceived to be in your way. It's mandatory in life to have a way of living that allows you peace of mind, confidence, and enjoyment. Your mind will surely perceive obstacles and problems without a Process, so don't be afraid to learn something that will change your life for the better.

RECAP OF THE PROCESS

1) Pre-Shot routine is the *Engine* that drives the Process. Repetition is the key to success in the game of golf and the proper routine is essential for successful repetition. It's not the content of your routine that's vital but what is vital is that you do the same thing EVERY time. Assess your situation using the rule of 1000 if necessary. Select your club with confidence. Use 5 Sense Imagery to create the shot in your mind. Use one, two, or three rehearsal swings to exactly replicate the shot you imagined. Address the ball and ask yourself if you're ready to go and only proceed if the answer is "Yes". Take one last look at the target and pull the trigger. If the answer to "Am I ready to hit this shot?" is "No", start your routine over again and do it until the answer is "Yes". All this sounds like it takes a lot of time, but once you've done

it consistently for a few weeks you should be able to go through your whole routine in a matter of seconds.

2) Acceptance is the *Heart* of the Process. Learn to accept whatever the outcome might be. You really have no control over what happens once the club makes contact with the ball, so wherever it goes, find it and proceed with your next shot. Stay in the moment, because that is the only place you can live your life. What just happened or what could happen are unimportant, only what you have in front of you in this moment is what truly matters. Have patience with the situation and yourself, and things will appear to be simpler, more organized, and fun. Patience is a learned trait and requires work but once it is achieved it will make life easier. There is no such thing as luck, and superstitions are useless. Accept responsibility for all actions and you'll keep your power. Blaming others or whining about your situation takes your power away. Things happen for an easily explained reasons so proceed with confidence in the moment, as you may have just placed yourself in a position for

greatness. Give up the need to control the situation because there really is no control of anything, except maybe how you feel or deal with your emotions in a given situation.

3) Focus is the *Backbone* of the Process. 5 Sense Imagery is the use of all five senses to imagine the shot about to be played. Once you've developed the ability to use all five senses you'll will have the intensity required to block out all distractions and create a tunnel vision-like focus. It's the conscious mind that guides the backswing and the subconscious mind that guides the approach into and through the contact zone. If your subconscious is confident and sure, your stroke will be fluid and aggressive. If your subconscious holds doubts or insecurities your stroke will be shaky and passive. Self-hypnosis and meditation can be used as a helpful tool to create positive feelings in your subconscious and strengthen your conscious mind. Staying in the present is one of the most difficult things to do in golf or life. Learn to stay in the present to keep your power. Thoughts of what just

happened or what could possibly happen only help to remove you from the intense focus required to succeed in any given moment. Once you learn to live in the moment you will be able to easily access *the Zone,* which is not a magical place but can only be accessed through intense *in the moment* focus. Be aware of your *self talk* as it is the image you reveal to the world of exactly how you feel about yourself. Learn to be more forgiving of yourself, as this is a difficult game and beating yourself up will only make the game tougher. Development of your focus and a solid overall Process will give you the confidence to avoid the dreaded *Yips,* which are an affliction that manifests itself in the subconscious. It's in your subconscious where negative thoughts fester. They are like little soldiers which get in your head and dig trenches. Once entrenched in your head they whistle for all their other little buddies to come join them and the next thing you know, your head is filled with negative thoughts. Usually someone with a head full of negative thoughts isn't even aware of it, but it is obvious to all those around that there is a problem. So remember, things sometimes do go wrong. There are just so many obstacles in the game that you must proceed to the next shot with the knowledge that your Process is strong enough to prevail over any situation.

4) Golfing your ball is the *Art* of the Process. The game of golf begins before you've hit your first shot, so prepare yourself for your next round as soon as the previous round has ended. Go to the range or practice green if you need to or just get some rest for the next day. Set your equipment specifically to meet your game, body, and your swing. Only make changes if the technology absolutely mandates it. Once your clubs are to your liking, take the time to learn all the skill shots that you may encounter in a round of golf. Work on moving the ball in all directions. Hit high and low shots, fades and draws, and take a seven iron and hit shots from 80 yards up to full swings. Learn to love the adverse weather conditions as most players don't. Go play in the wind, rain, heat, and cold as often as you can. In the wind, don't alter your game too much. Only hit shots that

you've practiced. In the rain never try to hit full shots. Success in the rain happens with solid contact and that can only happen with about a three quarter golf swing. Before you play the course, make sure you have a strategy and try to stick to it. The game has changed and strategy, though still needed, has become less important to most players. Because of the equipment and/or the modern day golfer's strength, most golf courses of the past have been rendered obsolete. Major tournaments or very difficult golf courses though, still require a solid strategy. Consistency and stability are essential for longevity in the game. Try to keep an even keel and avoid the emotional roller coasters that lead to over excitement or depression. Stoically go about your business and raise a fist in triumph only after you raise the trophy. Understanding the difference between expectations and intentions is critical to success. Expectations are future thoughts attached to the outcome. Intentions are your goals for the moment that are detached from the outcome. When you are attached to the outcome you'll end up frustrated when things don't go your way. Having an expectation can be a slippery slope that leads to negative thinking. Intentions are your desires offered to the universe that are unconcerned with the outcome. It's only your intention to make a putt but if it doesn't happen to go in, you are accepting of the result and may proceed with confidence to the next shot. Having *Selective Memory* will be helpful to forget when things don't go as planned. Usually what's happened in the past is best left in the past and having the ability to move forward undaunted by the past, is key to a successful future. Sometimes it's just as important to forget something wonderful that has just happened because from great heights come great falls. Stay consistent and even keeled to avoid the pitfalls of the roller coaster. Roller coasters can be fun but to live your life on one becomes nerve racking and exhausting. All that being said, there is something for taking chances when the situation calls for it. Once in a while it's necessary to throw caution to the wind, if for no other reason than to push your limits or to show that you have the courage to trust yourself in a challenging moment. Which leads me to probably the most crucial trait any golfer can possess, trust. Trust in your ability and a belief that your are prepared for any situation can be the difference between the player holding the trophy and the player you might never have heard of.

5) Finally, Off Course Management is the *Maintenance* of the Process. Like I said, preparation is the key to success in golf and life. Success does NOT happen without off course preparation. Fitness and nutrition are now mandatory at the PGA Tour level. The burdens of the game require today's player to be fitter, healthier, and possessing of more stamina than ever before. If you're not strengthening your body and mind every day, you're being lapped by all the other players who most definitely are. Trust me, today's professional golfer is so much more athletically gifted and physically fit than the players of even just ten years ago. They hit the ball much farther and have more stamina, so if you want to be competitive you must be ready to change your fitness and nutritional behavior. You must also learn

to manage your time. There are many skills, relationships, and mental and physical training that need to be developed to reach the top in this game, so you must use your time wisely. Get organized and prioritize what's most important to you in your life. Don't be afraid to lose wasteful habits like too much TV watching but always make time for reading. Be honest to all those who you choose to put in your life. They must be aware that you have a dream and that nothing or no one can deter you from achieving that dream. Make sure that the relationships you do have are with positive and supportive people who believe in you and your dreams. A good companion can make all the difference in your life but so can a bad companion. Through a devoted practice of the Process you'll learn to be the same person on and off the course. This will help benefit you to not only be a better golfer but a happier and healthier person. Integrity, courage, honesty, ethics, and compassion are just some of the traits of the Process oriented person. Try *Act as if* to help implant positive thoughts into your subconscious. Work at it everyday and soon you won't need it because with enough *acting* you'll begin to actually believe it's true. Be aware of the trap of swing mechanics. I'm not saying it isn't important to work on your swing but once your swing is working for you, have the courage to focus your attention on the Process and trust that your swing will work. Believe that the work you've put in on your swing will make it effective in crunch time. Remember, golf swings don't hold up under pressure, golfers do. It's my belief that the golfers who do have the unwavering belief in their abilities are the one's with the *It factor*. They are the golfers you watch on TV and think, "Wow, that player really has his act together" and you just know he's going to hang on and finish on top. They are the people you could pick out of a large crowd because they just seem to have something about them that produces a glowing aura. They are confident but not cocky and just have an intangible quality that elevates them to the top of whatever endeavor they participate in. Learn the Process and I assure you that if followed, these mental training methods and principles will radically improve your game. In fact, I believe that you will also notice a change in your life for the better. Life will seem easier and less stressful and if you've lost the love for the game that you once possessed, the Process is the answer to finding that love again.

It's my goal for this book that it be used by golfers or anyone who wants to improve their game and their life. It's my belief that the Process will work for any sport or profession if you simply replace the golf scenarios with whatever relates to your specific task.
I work with young and old, male or female, from Tour players to the weekend hacker, and I want to help you no matter what category you fall into.

For more information or to contact me, please visit my website at www.jonlevittgolf.com.